MICHIGAN LAW
FOR TEENAGERS

Bruce Micheals

Copyright © by Bruce Micheals

All rights reserved. No part of this book may be reproduced in any form for any reason without express written permission from the author.

Acknowledgement

I want to thank Bruce C. Micheals, Sr., for giving me this brilliant book idea and the motivation to pursue it. Thanks Dad.

For a safer, happier, and healthier society

Introduction

American teenagers face peer pressure to commit crimes that previous generations seldom if ever thought about. Due to advances in technology, American teenagers are regularly exposed to portrayals of criminal conduct that often glamorizes crime. From the portrayals of crime, the teens then form inaccurate opinions of what constitutes criminal behavior and the consequences of that behavior. As a result, more teens than ever are being processed into the criminal justice system. The teens often struggle to understand why their ideas of law and the system do not reflect what they are experiencing. Only years later do they come to understand that they never really understood the law as a teenager; by then, however, much of their youth has been lost to the effects of having a criminal record.

Michigan Law for Teenagers is intended to give teenagers a clear explanation of what constitutes many of the most common crimes that today's teenagers face. No attempt to scare the reader or exaggerate the law has been made. *Michigan Law for Teenagers* quotes, paraphrases, and summarizes Michigan law as it actually is. By using this approach, *Michigan Law for Teenagers* lets the law speak for itself. Teens can benefit from this concise and direct approach because they will quickly get the facts about the laws under which they live, without having to spend hundreds of hours in legal studies.

Table of Contents

Acknowledgement 3
Introduction 5
1. Assault 9
2. Breaking and Entering 35
3. Controlled Substances 57
4. Firearms and Other Weapons 93
5. Homicide 123
6. Larceny 147
7. Stolen, Embezzled, or Converted Property ... 177
8. Malicious and Wilful Mischief and Destruction 197
9. Miscellaneous Offenses 219
10. Prostitution and Human Trafficking 269
11. Rape and Criminal Sexual Conduct 289
12. Robbery 313
Appendix 341
Attention Reader 343

1.

Assault

Chapter 1 Basic Assault 11

Chapter 2 Serious or Aggravated Assault (w/o Weapon) 17

Chapter 3 Serious or Aggravated Assault (w/weapon) 19

Chapter 4 Assault w/Intent I 21

Chapter 5 Assault w/ Intent II 23

Chapter 6 Assault on a Pregnant Person 27

Notes 29

Index 31

Chapter 1

Basic Assault

1. What does the law say about assault?

"[A] person who assaults or assaults and batters an individual...is guilty of a misdemeanor punishable by imprisonment for not more than 93 days or a fine of not more than $500.00, or both."[1]

2. What is the difference between assault and battery?

The definition of assault is "[a]n unlawful threat or attempt to do bodily injury to another," and the definition of battery is "[t]he unlawful and unwanted touching or striking of one person by another, with the intention of bringing about a harmful or offensive contact."[2] However, the terms are often used interchangably.

3. What happens if I break the law?

You gamble with your safety, freedom, and prospects for the future. You also gamble with other people's lives, people who may be innocent, love you, or wish you no harm.

4. Do the punishments change depending on who is assaulted?

Yes. "[A]n individual who assaults or assaults and batters his or her spouse or former spouse, an individual with whom he or she has or has had a dating relationship, an individual with whom he or she has had a child in common, or a resident or former resident of his or her household, is guilty of a misdemeaner punishable by imprisonment for not more than 93 days or a fine of not more than $500.00, or both."[3] This special emphasis on people who had or have had close relationships is relevant because the punishments for assaulting such people increases significantly as the number of assaults increases.

5. Are special protections provided for pregnant people?

Yes. If an individual assaults or assaults and batters someone who is pregnant, that individual "is guilty of a misdemeaner punishable by imprisonment for not more than 93 days or a fine of not more than $500.00, or both."[4] The punishment for assaulting pregnant people also increases significantly as the number of assaults increases.

6. How do the punishments increase for assaults against one of the people listed in 5 and 6 above?

A second conviction for assault or assault and battery against those people increases the misdemeanor punishment to "imprisonment for not more than 1 year or a fine of not more than $1,000.00, or both."[5]

7. If the second assault can get me four times as much time in jail as the first assault, how much time would I be facing if I got a third assault?

"An individual who commits an assault or an assault and battery [against someone from 5 or 6 above] and who has two or more previous convictions for assaulting or assaulting and battering [of that kind] is guilty of a felony punishable by imprisonment for not more than 5 years or a fine of not more than $5,000.00, or both."[6]

8. Are there any assault laws specifically related to police officers?

Yes. Special laws do apply to police officers, conservation officers, sheriffs, deputy sherrifs, constables, secret service agents and other peace officers, firefighters, emergency medical service personnel, and people engaged in search and rescue operations.[7] The law states that "an individual who assaults, batters, wounds, resists, obstructs, opposes, or endangers a person who the individual knows or has reason to know is performing his or her duties is guilty of a felony punishable by imprisonment for not more than 2 years or a fine of not more than $2,000.00, or both."[8] If the offense causes the person "bodily injury requiring medical attention or medical care [the individual] is guilty of a felony punishable by imprisonment for not more than 4 years or a fine of not more than $5,000.00, or both."[9] If the offense causes the person "a serious impairment of a body function [the individual] is guilty of a felony punishable by imprisonment for not more than 15 years or a fine of not more than $10,000.00, or both."[10] If the offense causes the person to die [the individual] "is guilty of a felony punishable by imprisonment for not more than 20 years or a fine of not more than $20,000.00, or both."[11] Another important part of the law concerning offenses against the above listed public servants is that the sentence can be "run consecutively to any term of imprisonment imposed for another violation arising from the same transaction."[12] This means the judge can make the sentence, for an offense against a listed public servant, to be served before or after any other sentences that one might otherwise have to serve. For example, suppose a police officer tries to cuff a person for a relatively minor fight, and that person resists the officer's attempt to secure the cuffs around the person's wrists. The person, if found guilty, can be sentenced to up to 93 days imprisonment for the fight and up to an additional 2 years for resisting the officer.

CHAPTER 2

SERIOUS OR AGGRAVATED ASSAULT (W/O WEAPON)

9. What does the law say about more serious assaults than those covered in chapter 1?

"A person who assaults an individual without a weapon and inflicts serious or aggravated injury upon that individual without intending to commit murder or to inflict great bodily harm less than murder is guilty of a misdemeanor punishable by imprisonment for not more than 1 year or a fine of not more than $1,000.00, or both."[13]

10. Does the punishment change, like the one did in chapter 1, depending on who is assaulted?

Yes. The punishment changes when the class of people listed in answer 5 of chapter 1 (i.e., people with whom one had or has had a close relationship) are involved more than once. The law states that an individual with "1 or more previous convictions for assaulting or assaulting and battering [a person in this category] is guilty of a felony punishable by imprisonment for not more than 5 years or a fine of not more than $5,000.00, or both."[14] Note:This segment of law does not address multiple assaults on pregnant people; however, we will pick up the topic again in chapter 6.

Chapter 3

Serious or Aggravated Assault (w/weapon)

11. What is Felonious Assault?

Felonious assault is essentially using a weapon to commit the same crime as described in answer 8 of chapter 2. The law says that "a person who assaults another person with a gun, revolver, pistol, knife, iron bar, club, brass knuckles, or other dangerous weapon without intending to commit murder or to inflict great bodily harm less than murder is guilty of a felony punishable of imprisonment for not more than 4 years or a fine of not more than $2,000.00, or both."[15]

12. Does the punishment change, here too, depending on who is assaulted?

No. The punishment does change, however, if the felony assault occurs at a school, on school property, or in a weapon free school zone. This means virtually any school building, school property, school event, or school vehicle used to transport students is protected. The sentence for felony assault at one of these locations is the same 4 years imprisonment, as cited above, however, the judge has an additional option of sentencing offenders to up to 150 hours of community service or a fine of up to $6,000.00.[16]

CHAPTER 4

ASSAULT W/INTENT I

13. What is Assault with Intent?

Assault with intent is a reference to several different laws related to assaults that occur while the perpetrator has specific intentions.

14. What is an example of an Assault with Intent law?

Assault with intent to commit felony, not otherwise punished is an example of such a law. With this law a "person who shall assault another, with intent to commit any burglary, or any other felonyshall be guilty of a felony, punishable by imprisonment in the state prison not more than 10 years, or by fine of not more than $5,000.00."[17]

15. Does the punishment change depending on the intent?

Yes. For instance, an unarmed person who assaults someone as part of a burglary (see 13 above) will face up to 10 years in prison; however, if that unarmed person assaults someone with an intent to rob them, the punishment is imprisonment for not more than

15 years.[18] The sentence increases to any number of years, up to life in prison, for Assault with Intent to Rob and Steal [while] Being Armed.[19] So, for example, pulling a gun out and telling someone, "give me your money, or I am going to shoot you" is enough to send someone to prison for any number of years. The threat and presence of anything that might make someone believe the threat can in fact be carried out is enough to convict someone of Assault with Intent to Rob [while] Armed.[20]

16. How can anyone know what someone else intends?

Defendents in intent related cases often try to raise the defense that they did not have the intent to commit the crime, which means they can be found not guilty of that crime if they can persuade a jury to agree with them. Typically, "proof of specific intent, [is] inferred from the circumstances."[21] That means the jury will decide whether they think a given activity or behavior indicates someone possessed an intent to rob, or whatever the intent element of the crime happens to be, based on the circumstances or context that the activity or behavior occur in.

Chapter 5

Assault w/ Intent II

17. What does the law say about assault with intent to commit murder?

"Any person who shall assault another with intent to commit the crime of murder, shall be guilty of a felony, punishable by imprisonment in the state prison for life or any number of years."[22] Assault with intent to murder has two elements: (1) that the defendant assaulted the victim and (2) that at the time of the assault the defendant intended to murder the victim.[23]

18. If I was charged with assault with intent to murder, couldn't I get out of it simply by saying that I never intended to kill anyone?

No. If you are tried for assault with intent to murder, a jury will consider what you did and the circumstances that were occuring at the time that you did them, and they will decide for themselves whether they believe you intended to murder someone when you assaulted them.[24]

19. A friend of mine got into a fight, and he got mad and started choking the other guy and saying "I'll kill you!" But he didn't really mean that he would actually kill the guy. Is that "simple assault" or assault with intent to murder?

Your description sounds like assault with intent to do great bodily harm less than murder. The law states that, "A person who does either of the following is guilty of a felony punishable by imprisonment for not more than 10 years or a fine of not more than $5,000.00, or both: (a) Assaults another person with intent to do great bodily harm, less than the crime of murder. (b) Assaults another person by strangulation or suffocation."[25]

20. If my friend had not actually said "I'll kill you!" could he still have been shown to have intent to do great bodily harm less than murder?

Your friend's statement is not nearly as important as the fact that his hands were around the other person's neck strangling him. Remember this: "threat may be made by conduct as well as by words."[26] That means one's intent can be understood by thinking about the actions they take such as how they stand, what they hold in their hands , how they approach others, the expression on their face, and how they use objects. For example, if you were to pull a knife out of your pocket when someone came to start a fight with you, you--not the other person-- would be facing a 10 year prison sentence for assault with intent to do great bodily harm less than murder. Why? Because pulling out a knife while being threatened, indicates an intent to stab or cut someone.

21. What is the law against intentionally trying to maim someone?

Assault with Intent to Maim. That law states that assaulting someone with the intent to maim or disfigure them is "a felony, punishable by imprisonment in the state prison for not more than 10 years or by fine of not more than $5,000.00."[27] This means activities such as poking an eye out, cutting an ear, nose, or lip, and disabling a limb, organ, or member are punishable by up to 10 years in prison. Another law called Mayhem reads almost exactly the same as assault with intent to maim, except mayhem includes everyone else who was present and knew of the person's intent to do the maiming and aided in it--even if the aiding is as minor as holding a door open, driving the perpetrator to the scene, or supplying a weapon. The punishment for mayhem is the same as for assault with intent to maim: up to 10 years in prison or not more than a fine of $5,000.00.[28]

22. Isn't maiming and torture the same?

No, but they are similar. Both crimes include an intent to severely injure another person. However, torture takes it steps further: (1) the perpetrator's intent is to "cause cruel or extreme physical or mental pain and suffering" [in addition to the bodily injury] and (2) the victim is in the perpetrator's custody or physical control. This felony is punishable by imprisonment for life or any number of years.[29]

CHAPTER 6

ASSAULT ON A PREGNANT PERSON

23. How is an assault on a pregnant person different than an assault on anyone else?

By law, "if a person intentionally [assaults a pregnant person with the intention] to cause a miscarriage or still birth or death...or great bodily harm to the embryo or fetus, and the person's conduct result[s] in a miscarriage or stillbirth...or death to the embryo or fetus" the person is guilty of a felony punishable by imprisonment for life or any term of years. The law also states that the person is guilty if he or she "act[s] in wanton or willful disregard of the likelihood that the natural tendency of the person's conduct is to cause a miscarriage or stillbirth or death or great bodily harm to the embryo or fetus."[30]

24. What does that mean?

It means, if you assault a pregnant person you can get life in prison for killing or damaging an unborn baby. It also means that you can get life in prison for doing something foolish to a pregnant person if that foolish act results in the death or damage to the unborn baby.

25. Are there any exceptions to the life sentence?

There are some other laws regarding assaults and cases of gross negligence, on pregnant people, that result in miscarriage or stillborn or death to the embryo or fetus. These laws are punishable by imprisonment for not more than 15 years or a fine of not more than $7,500.00, or both. The punishment decreases from there in stages depending on the damage to the embryo or fetus. The least damage calls for "a misdemeanor punishable by imprisonment for not more than 93 days or a fine of not more than $500.00, or both."[31]

Notes

1. MCLS 750.81(1) This is the Michigan law at the date of this publication.

2. The American Heritage College Dictionary, 4ed., (Joseph P. Pickett et al. eds., Houghton Mifflin Company. Boston 2002.)

3. MCLS 750.81(2)

4. MCLS 750.81(3)

5. MCLS 750.81(4)

6. MCLS 750.81(5)

7. MCLS 750.81d (7)(b)(i-x)

8. MCLS 750.81d (1)

9. MCLS 750.81d (2)

10. MCLS 750.81d (3)

11. MCLS 750.81d (4)

12. MCLS 750.81d (6)

13. MCLS 750.81a (1)

14. MCLS 750.81a (3)

15. MCLS 750.82 (1)

16. MCLS 750.82 (2-3)

17. MCLS 750.87

18. MCLS 750.88

20. People v. Johnson, 130 Mich. App. 26, 1983 Mich. App. LEXIS 3383 (Mich. Ct. App. 1983) (The elements of the specific intent crime of assault with intent to rob while armed are (1) an assault (2) committed with a dangerous weapon or an article used or fashioned to lead the individual assaulted to reasonably believe it to be a dangerous weapon (3) by a defendant possessing the intent to rob and steal.)

21. People v. Harris, 110 Mich. App. 636, 1981 Mich. App. LEXIS 3366 (Mich. Ct. App. 1981).

22. MCLS 750.83

23. People v. Smith, 119 Mich. App.91, 1982 Mich. App. LEXIS 3442 (Mich. Ct. App. 1982)

24. People v. Newton, 152 Mich. App. 630, 1987 Mich. LEXIS 7059 (Mich.1987).

25. MCLS 750.84

26. People v. Counts, 318 Mich. 45, 1947 Mich. LEXIS 368 (Mich. 1947).

27. MCLS 750.86

28. MCLS 750.397

29. MCLS 750.85

30. MCLS 750.90a

31. MCLS 750.90b and MCLS 750.90c

INDEX

Index numbers refer to question numbers, not to page numbers.

aggravated assault (See assault, aggravated)

aggravated injury (See injury, aggravated)

aided: 21

assault: 1, 2, 4-8, 10-15, 17-21, 23-25

--aggravated: 9

--felonious: 11, 12

--first: 7

--second: 7

--serious: 9

--third: 7

--with intent: 13, 14

--with intent to commit felony: 14

--with intent to commit murder: 17-19

--w/intent to commit great bodily harm less than murder: 19, 20

--with intent to maim: 21

--with intent to rob: 15

--with intent to rob while armed: 15

battery: 1, 2, 4-7, 10

bodily injury (See injury, bodily)
burglary: 14, 15
cause of death: 8
child in common: 4
choking: 19
close relationship: 10
consecutive sentence: 8
conservation officer: 8
constable: 8
damage to the embryo or fetus: 25
dangerous weapon: 11
dating relationship: 4
death to the embryo or fetus: 23, 25
deputy sheriff: 8
disfigure: 21
emergency medical service personnel: 8
felonious assault (See assault, felonious)
felony: 7, 8, 10-12, 14, 17, 19, 21, 22
fight: 19, 20
firefighter: 8
first assault (See assault, first)
great bodily harm to the embryo or fetus: 23

gross negligence: 25
gun: 11
"I'll kill you!": 19, 20
injury: 8
--aggravated: 43
--bodily: 8, 22
--serious: 9, 22
intent: 15, 16, 20-22 (See also assault)
knife: 20
maim: 21, 22
mayhem: 21
miscarriage: 23, 25
misdemeanor: 1, 6, 9, 25
peace officer: 8
physical control: 22
police officer: 8
pregnant people: 5, 10, 23-25
previous convictions: 7, 10
proof of intent: 16
public servant: 8
school: 12
--property: 12

--vehicle: 12

secret service agent: 8

second assault (See assault, second)

second conviction: 6

serious assault (See assault serious)

serious impairment: 8

serious injury (See injury, serious)

sheriff: 8

spouse: 4

stillbirth: 23, 25

strangulation: 19, 20

suffocation: 19

third assault (See assault, third)

threat: 15, 20 (See also "I'll kill you!")

torture: 22

unborn baby: 24

victim: 22

wanton or wilful disregard: 23

weapon: 11

weapon free school zone: 12

2.

Breaking and Entering

Chapter 1 Home Invasion 37

Chapter 2 Breaking and Entering 41

Chapter 3 Burglary w/Explosives 45

Chapter 4 Entering w/o Breaking 49

Notes 51

Index 53

Chapter 1

Home Invasion

1. What is home invasion?

The law says that "a person who breaks and enters a dwelling [a residence or attached structure] with intent to commit a felony, larceny, or assault in the dwelling, a person who enters a dwelling without permission with intent to commit a felony, larceny, or assault in the dwelling, or a person who breaks and enters a dwelling or enters without permission and, at any time while he or she is entering, present in, or exiting the dwelling, commits a felony, larceny, or assault is guilty of home invasion in the first degree if at any time while the person is entering, present in, or exiting the dwelling either of the following circumstances exist: (a) The person is armed with a dangerous weapon. (b) Another person is lawfully present in the dwelling."[1] First degree home invasion is "punishable by imprisonment for not more than 20 years or a fine of not more than $5,000.00, or both."[2]

2. What does all that mean?

If, without permission, you carry anything that can be used as a weapon into someone's house, garage, basement, or other area of the building that they live at, and someone else is legally there--whether you know it or not--and you commit a felony, steal something, or assault anyone at any time while there, you will be facing up to 20 years in prison for first degree home invasion.

3. What is second degree home invasion?

The same as first degree home invasion minus the two elements, a and b, listed in the answer to question 1. In other words, you will be guilty of second degree home invasion if you commit a felony, larceny, or assault in someone's dwelling if you do not have permission to be there. For second degree you do not have to have a weapon and the dwelling can be unoccupied.[3] The punishment for second degree home invasion is "imprisonment for not more than 15 years or a fine of not more than $3,000.00, or both."[4]

4. Is there a third degree home invasion?

Yes. It involves either entering a dwelling, without permission, with the intent to commit a misdemeanor or entering a dwelling and violating any of the following: "(i) A probation term or condition, (ii) A parole term or condition, (iii) A personal protection order term or condition, (iv) A bond or bail condition or any condition of pretrial release."[5] The punishment for third degree home invasion is "imprisonment for not more than 5 years or a fine of not more than $2,000.00, or both."[6]

Third degree [not second degree] home invasion [is] a necessar[y] included lesser offense of first degree home invasion. [7] That means, people who go to trial may be found guilty of third degree home invasion if the first degree cannot be proven beyond a reasonable doubt. This is worth knowing because many other crimes use this principle too. A person is charged with a given crime and throughout the trial the person defends against the elements of that crime only to be found guilty of a lesser included offense, which is simply a similar but easier to prove crime.

CHAPTER 2

BREAKING AND ENTERING

5. What is breaking and entering?

The law states that "A person who breaks and enters, with intent to commit a felony or a larceny therein, a tent, hotel, office, store, shop, warehouse, barn, granary, factory, or other building, structure, boat, ship, shipping container, or railroad car is guilty of a felony punishable by imprisonment for not more than 10 years."[8]

6. What does "breaking" mean?

To break as it applies to breaking and entering, the use of force to open a door or window or other entrance is necessary.[9] The amount of force is irrelevant, however, because the use of any force at all...is sufficient to constitute the element of breaking and entering.[10] Breaking, as it applies to the elements of breaking and entering, does not mean destroying property. Breaking in this sense means moving. For example, in People v. Hill, the defendant "had pushed aside an already opened door [and doing was] sufficient to constitute a breaking."[11]

7. How can anyone ever be found guilty of breaking and entering if intent has to be proved?

"Under Michigan law, intent...may be inferred from totality of circumstances as nature, time or place of defendant's acts before and during breaking and entering."[12] This means the jury, during trial, is allowed to guess at what the defendant's intent was before and during the breaking and entering, based on the information provided at the trial.

Determining intent isn't a pure science; instead, members of the jury are tasked with trying to figure out what a person's intent was during a given offense. Sometimes they get it correct, and other times they get it wrong. Citizens are tasked with avoiding the mere hint of illegal behavior. Because law is not an exact science, people should take reasonable measures to ensure that their behavior is difficult to interpret as illegal. A good way to do that is simply (1) to avoid questionable conduct and (2) to explain our actions to causal observers, so they will not draw negative conclusions.

8. If someone breaks into a house while the owner is gone, is that punishable by up to 10 years--like any other breaking and entering?

No. Breaking into places where people live is called home invasion, which, assuming the perpetrator did not have a weapon, would carry up to 15 years (see chapter 1, question 3).

9. In the crime of breaking and entering, are you guilty of "entering" if you only put one finger in the doorway or window?

Yes. Entering does not require one's entire body to "enter." By law, one is guilty as soon as any part of their person enters.[13]

CHAPTER 3

BURGLARY W/EXPLOSIVES

10. What is burglary with explosives?

Any entering of a building "for the purpose of committing any crime therein" and using or attempting to use a high explosive is a felony, punishable by imprisonment in the state prison not less less than15 years nor more than 30 years."[14]

11. Why would the sentence be a minimum of 15 years?

Because the law makers, in 1931, wanted to make sure the people who were using explosives during burglaries got long prison sentences that they could not get out of if they were convicted.

12. But what if someone breaks into someone's shed and lights a pipebomb?

That simple prank, perhaps funny to a teenager, places the authorities in a very difficult position because n law if the teen waived over into the adult system and found guilty of the crime, the judge has to sentence the teen to at least 15 years in prison.

13. That's not fair; it was just a joke or at worst a mean act of destruction to property.

This book is being published specifically because of the unfairness that you are referring to. Before juveniles were waived into the adult system, this 15 year minimum punishment was not applied to them. Now, however, an unknown number of juveniles have faced it and have presumably been sent to prison. Hopefully, after reading this book, the reader will be less likely to engage in activities that may subject them to adult punishments.

14. A friend of mine made a device for breaking into locks; is that against the law?

That depends on the intent your friend has for using the device. "Any person who shall have in his possession any [explosive], engine, machine, tool or implement, device, chemical or substance, adapted or designed for cutting or burning through, forcing or breaking open any building, room, vault, or safe or other depository, in order to steal therefrom [while] knowing the same to be adapted or designed for the purpose aforesaid, with intent to use or employ the same for the purpose aforesaid, shall be guilty of a felony, punishable by imprisonment in the state prison not more than 10 years."[15]

15. The word intent is used in this law too. How does it relate to possession of burglar's tools?

The primary element of burglar's tools are "[1] that the tool or implement be adapted or designed for breaking and entering; [2] that it be in the possession of one who has knowledge that it is adapted and designed for that purpose; and [3] that it be possessed with intent to use or employ it in breaking and entering."[16] This possession of an item with intent to use it in a breaking and entering might be as simple as possessing a crowbar.[17] For the person who intends to use the crowbar to illegally gain entry to other people's buildings, rooms, or other locked property, the possession of a crowbar is a felony punishable by up to 10 years in prison.

16. How can other people know your intent though?

They cannot. No one can absolutely know the intent of another person. However, that does not matter because juries only have to infer intent. That means the jury is asked to use common sense while listening to the evidence presented at trial, and through the use of common sense, they are asked to give their opinion as to whether the accused person had the intent to commit an illegal act. By law, the jury does not have to be sure of one's intent; they just have to provide their best guess. So, for example, possession of a chisel and flashlight outside of a place that had just been burglarized was enough to send a man to prison for both breaking and entering and possession of burglary tools.[18]

17. Almost anything can be used to commit a breaking and entering though. How can anyone be safe from prosecution?

Common household items alone is not sufficient to uphold a conviction for possession of burglary tools: "where there is no evidence in the record and no circumstance disclosed warranting an inference that defendant possessed them for the purpose of breaking and entering, a conviction will be reversed."[19] In People v. Murphy, the "term 'adapted and designed'...means something more then mere common household articles capable of use in breaking and entering."[20]

The focus, as you can see, is not that almost anything can be used to commit breaking and entering but that it is illegal to possess things for the purpose of committing a breaking and entering. This distinction can be difficult to grasp, but people who do not involve themselves in any criminal activity do not usually have any problem with it.

Chapter 4

Entering w/o Breaking

18. A friend of mine knows this place where you can go inside and steal stuff, but you don't have to open a door or window to get in there. Is that still breaking and entering or is it stealing [larceny]?

From your description, it sounds like the law of entering without breaking, which reads, "Any person who, without breaking, enters any dwelling, house, tent, hotel, office, store, shop, warehouse, barn, granary, factory, or other building, boat, ship, shipping container, railroad car or structure used or kept for public or private use, or any private apartment therein, with intent to commit a felony or an larceny therein, is guilty of a felony punishable by imprisonment for not more than 5 years or a fine of not more than $2,500.00."[21]

19. So it is entering without breaking if I go into an open building or container , of almost any sort, with the intent to commit a felony or steal something?

Yes. That is exactly what the law means. Some buildings and containers are left open at certain times, and stealing from them can be very easy; however, dowing so puts you at risk of being found guilty of a felony and spending up to 5 years in prison.

20. Why is the fine only $2,500.00 when the prison sentence is 5 years?

This law was made in 1931. At that time $2,500.00 was a large amount of money. Today, if given a choice, most people would probably choose a $2,500.00 fine over 5 years in prison. However, defendants are not given a choice at sentencing.

NOTES

1. MCLS 750.110a (2)

2. MCLS 750.110a (5)

3. MCLS 750.110a (3)

4. MCLS 750.110a (6)

5. MCLS 750.110a (4)

6. MCLS 750.110a (7)

7. People v. Wilder, 485 Mich. 35, 2010 Mich. LEXIS 471 (Mich. 2010).

8. MCLS 750.110 (1)

9. People v. Kedo, 108 Mich. App. 310, 1981 Mich. App. LEXIS 3181 (Mich. Ct. App. 1981).

10. People v. Finney, 113 Mich. App. 638, 1982 Mich. App. LEXIS 2964 (Mich. Ct. App. 1982).

11. People v. Hill, 36 Mich. App. 679, 1971 Mich. App. LEXIS 1360 (Mich. Ct. App. 1971).

12. Goldman v. Anderson, 625 F.2d, 135, 1980 U.S. App. LEXIS 15394 (6th Cir. Mich. 1980).

13. People v. Gillman, 66 Mich. App. 419, 1976 Mich. App. LEXIS 1203 (Mich. Ct. App. 1976).

14. MCLS 750.112

15. MCLS 750.116

16. People v. Dorrington, 221 Mich. 571, 1923 Mich. LEXIS 500 (Mich. 1923).

17. People v. Gross, 118 Mich. App. 161, 1982 Mich. App. LEXIS 3343 (Mich. Ct. App. 1982).

18. People v. Ross, 39 Mich. App. 697, 1972 Mich. app. LEXIS 1521 (Mich. Ct. App. 1972).

19. People v. Dorrington, 221 Mich. 571, 1923 Mich. LEXIS 500 (MICH. 1923).

20. People v. Murphy, 28 Mich. App. 150, 1970 Mich. App. LEXIS 1133 (Mich. Ct. App. 1970).

21. MCLS 750.111

INDEX

Index numbers refer to question numbers, not to page numbers.

adapted: 17

assault: 1, 3

bail or bond condition: 4

breaking: 6 (See also "breaking and entering.")

breaking and entering: 1, 5-7, 15-17 (See also "breaking" and "entering.")

burglar's tools: 15-17

burglary: 11, 16

common sense: 16

crowbar: 15

dangerous weapon: 1

designed: 17

dwelling: 1, 3, 4, 18

elements of crime: 4

entering: 9, 10, 18 (See also "breaking and entering.")

entering without breaking: 18

evidence: 16

exact science: 7

explosives: 11, 14

felony: 1, 3, 5, 10, 15, 18, 19

first degree: 1-4 (See also "home invasion.")

flashlight: 16

force: 6

funny to a teenager: 12

high explosives: 10

home invasion: 1, 8 (See also "first degree", "second degree", "third degree")

inferred intent: 7, 16

intent: 1, 4, 5, 7, 14-16, 18

jury: 7, 16

"just a joke": 13

larceny: 1, 3, 5, 18

necessary included lesser offense: 4

parole: 4

personal protection order (PPO): 4

possession of burglar's tools: 15-17

possession of chisel: 16

prank: 12

probation: 4

pure science: 7

questionable conduct: 7

reasonable doubt: 4

residence: 1

safes: 11, 14

second degree: 3 (See also "home invasion.")

third degree: 4 (See also "home invasion.")

tool: 14, 15

totality of circumstances: 7

unfair: 13

unoccupied: 3

vault: 14

waived into adult system: 12, 13

weapon: 3, 8

without permission: 4

3.

Controlled Substances

Chapter 1 Making and Selling Drugs I 59

Chapter 2 Making and Selling Drugs II 69

Chapter 3 Making and Selling Counterfeit Drugs 75

Chapter 4 Possessing Drugs 77

Appendix Controlled Substances 81

Notes 85

Index 88

CHAPTER 1

MAKING AND SELLING DRUGS I

1. What happens if I break the law?

You gamble with your safety, freedom, and prospects for the future. You also gamble with other people's lives, people who may be innocent, love you, or wish you no harm.

2. But what will actually happen of I get caught for breaking a law?

After you are arrested, you will either go to the hospital or the county jail. If you go to the hospital, you probably got shot or otherwise injured during the arrest. Once you are released from the hospital, you will be transferred to the county jail or a juvenile facility if you are under 17 (See appendix A for information on Michigan's juvenile waiver law.)

For very minor violations, you will be detained for hours or days before being released for free or a small amount of money. For many other violations, you will be detained for several months, in the county jail, until you pay thousands of dollars in bail or go to trial or plead guilty. If you are found not guilty at trial, you will be released from jail. If you are found guilty or plea guilty, you will be sentenced by a judge.

3. What does the law say about making and/or selling drugs?

"[A] person shall not manufacture, create, deliver, or possess with intent to manufacture, create, or deliver a controlled substance, a prescription form, or a counterfeit prescription form." [1]

4. What does that mean?

It means that it is against the law to make drugs, give other people drugs, or have drugs that you plan to give to other people. It also means that it is illegal to have a prescription form or a fake prescription form.

5. What is the most that I could be sentenced to for making and selling drugs?

If you are dealing with with schedule 1 or 2 narcotics, those are "hard" drugs like heroin, you will be facing "imprisonment for life or any term of years or a fine of not more than $1,000,000.00, or both," for 1,000 grams or more. [2] (See Appendix B for information on schedule 1-5. Also, see question #42 for information on methamphetamines.)

6. That is a huge prison sentence and fine, but I don't plan to ever have 1,000 grams. What if I have less?

If you have "450 grams or more, but less than 1,000 grams," you will be facing "imprisonment for not more than 30 years or a fine of not more than $500,000.00, or both." [3]

7. That is still a lot of drugs. If I made or sold less, how much time in prison would I be facing if I got caught?

If you have "50 grams or more, but less than 450 grams," you will be facing "imprisonment for not more than 20 years or a fine of not more than $250,000.00, or both." [4]

8. I can definitely imagine myself dealing with 50 or more grams, but now that I know what the law is, I will always handle less than 50 grams. What is the law for less than 50 grams?

If you have "less than 50 grams," you will be facing "imprisonment for not more than 20 years or a fine of not more than $25,000.00, or both." [5]

9. So I can actually get sent to prison for up to 20 years if I make or sell any amount of schedule 1 or 2 narcotic?

Yes.

10. What if I only deal in non-narcotics?

Some drugs hold the same 20 years/$25,000.00 penalty as schedule 1 or 2 narcotics, but relatively small amounts of "other controlled substance[s]...except marihuana" [are]...punishable by imprisonment for not more than 7 years or a fine of not more than $10,000.00, or both." This law includes schedule 1, 2, and 3 drugsexcept marihuana. [6]

11. That can't be right: I know people who have been caught with drugs that they made or were selling, and they didn't get all that time. Why is there an inconsistency between what the law says and what I see?

I know people who have been given "light" sentences too. Judicial discretion is the authority judges sometimes exercise when they give offenders more or less time than the sentencing guidelines call for. The majority of America's 2.3 million prisoners have drug related crimes. Many of them believed judges would go easy on them if they hired a good lawyer, apologized tearfully, or begged for the court to be merciful. In prison today hundeds of thousands of people complain daily about how they got sent to prison for less than what other people got.

12. Maybe I can grow and sell marihuana instead of the hard drugs. What do the laws say about that?

Marihuana or any mixture containing marihuana that weighs "45 kilograms or more, or 200 plants or more," is punishable "by imprisonment for not more than 15 years or a fine of not more than $10,000,000.00, or both." [7]

Pay attention to the huge fine that is attached to the marihuana law. This fine is ten times larger than the largest fine for heroin. This fine ensures that people who try to illegally profit from the marihuana trade lose virtually all of the profits without necessarily spending the rest of their life in prison, as they might with other drugs.

13. I understand, but I'm not going to make 45 kilograms of edibles or raise 200 plants. What does the law say about dealing with smaller amounts?

If you have five kilograms or more but less than 45 kilograms, or 20 plants or more but fewer than 200 plants...[you will face] imprisonment for not more than 7 years or a fine of not more than $500,000.00, or both." [8]

14. A $500,000.00 fine for little more than a couple pounds of marihuana seems excessive to me, but I could probably still make money off of less marihuana. What does the law say?

If you have "less than 5 kilograms or fewer than 20 plants...[you will face] imprisonment for not more than 4 years or a fine of not more than $20,000.00, or both." [9]

15. So if I spend all of my time and money growing marihuana or making marihuana products, the authorities can just take it, fine me, and throw me in prison?

Yes.

16. Didn't the law change? I thought marihuana was practically legal now.

Marihuana is illegal; processing it for use by other people is a felony. [10] That means it is a crime to grow it, prune it, cultivate it, harvest it, dry it, cut it, mix it, package it, deliver it, give it, sell it, or otherwise participate in or conspire in the preparation of marihuana for use by others.

17. What about medical marihuana?

Medical marihuana is a very misunderstood and misused subject. We will discuss personal use and possession in chapter 4. As for using medical marihuana to make money, The federal Controlled Substance Act (CSA) prohibits it. [11] Numerous examples are available to support this; for instance, consider the following summary excerpt of a federal criminal appeal case.

"In a federal prosecution of a defendant for violating federal laws prohibiting the manufacturing and distribution of marihuana, the defendant, who was licensed under the Michigan Medical Marihuana Act to grow marihuana for up to five patients, precluded from introducing into evidence the defense medical necessity [or the] or the evidence that he was mistaken about the prospect of his activity violating federal law when he was in compliance with state law." [12]

In other words, even though the defendant had a Michigan Medical Marihuana Act license and had thought he was complying with the law, he was still prosecuted as any other drug dealer would be prosecuted. His license and ignorance of law were ineffective at protecting him from prosecution.

18. Maybe I can sell schedule 4 or 5 drugs instead of more risky ones. What does the law say about trying to deal in schedule 4 or 5 drugs?

You will be facing up to 4 years and/or a $2,000.00 fine for dealing in schedule 4 drugs. [13] As for schedule 5 drugs, you will face up to 2 years and/or a $2,000.00 fine. [14] However, the demand for schedule 4 and 5 drugs is relatively small. As you can read in Appendix B, schedule 4 and 5 drugs "[have] a low potential for abuse[.]" [15, 16] That means they will probably not be of much interest to people who want to get intoxicated.

19. Couldn't I just make or steal some prescription forms to get drugs that I can sell?

Anyone caught with "[a] prescription form or a counterfeit prescription form is guilty of a felony punishable by imprisonment for more than 7 years or a fine of not more than $5,000.00, or both." [17] This does not count the amount of time that you will get for the drugs if you actually use the prescription form.

20. I still feel like there is a lot of money to be made in the illegal drug trade. Why do I keep thinking about using drugs to make money?

Some people turn to making and selling drugs because (1) they do not know how else to acquire the amount of money that they desire or (2) they make and sell drugs as part of their lifestyle: either to pay for their drug habit or to be liked by people who use drugs.

21. How do I stop turning to the illegal drug trade to resolve my money problems or interests?

First, acknowledge that it is only a matter of time before you get caught. People are going to tell on you if you are committing crimes. The drug trade is infested with "snitches," and many people who get caught for crimes try to lessen their sentences by telling on other people. If you are in the drug trade, people will be telling on you, and you will get caught.

Second, once you understand that it is only a matter of time before you get caught, use the time that you have to get off of drugs. As long as your thinking is affected by drugs, you will struggle to grow beyond them. Go to AA/NA, talk to a school counselor, see a minister, check the Internet for drug hotlines that you can call, talk to a friend or family member who has recovered from drug abuse.

Third, find a mentor. A mentor is someone who will help you make your life better. Choose your mentor wisely. Look for a responsible, law-abiding person that you respect. Tell him or her that you are trying to figure out how to figure out how to make your life better, and ask for help. Some mentors are better than others, so always look for more mentors and people to learn from.

Chapter 2

Making and Selling Drugs II

22. Some of my friends want to pay me to let them use my garage. I didn't ask them why they wanted to use it; could I get in trouble if they are making drugs in there?

Yes. As owner or renter of the property, you are responsible for the activities that occur there. Claiming ignorance will not keep you out of prison. The law says you may not "[o]wn, possess, or use a vehicle, building, structure, place, or area that [you know] or [have reason to know] is to be used as a location to manufacture a controlled substance...or a counterfeit substance or a substance analogue in violation of section 7402." [18]

23. What does all that really mean?

It is illegal to own, rent, lease, or otherwise possess land or any structure in which people make or sell drugs.

24. My friends also want me to hold onto some of their chemicals and lab equipment. Is that illegal too?

Yes. The law says you may not "[o]wn or possess any chemical or any laboratory equipment that [you] or know[] or [have] reason to know is to be used for the purpose of manufacturing a controlled substance...or a counterfeit substance or a controlled substance analogue in violation of section 7402."[19]

25. And that means what?

It means your friends are asking you to hold stuff that can get you sent to prison.

26. They also want me to buy some chemicals and lab equipment for them. Can I get into trouble for buying them store products that are entirely legal?

Yes. As a citizen, you are expected to use common sense and discretion when dealing with other people. Note how the law here is worded: You may not "[p]rovide any chemical or laboratory equipment to another person knowing or having reason to know that the other person intends to use that chemical or laboratory equipment for the purpose of manufacturing a controlled substance...or a counterfeit substance or a controlled substance analogue in violation of section 7402." [20]

27. Does that mean that I am responsible for other people's actions?

It means that you will be held responsible if people make drugs with chemicals and lab equipment that you have given to them.

28. That isn't fair. I can't know what other people are going to do. How can anyone avoid being charged with a crime, under such strict laws?

Prison is full of people who complain about the laws being too broad and difficult to follow. Meanwhile, society is full of people who are either on their way to prison or following the rules that are required to keep them out of prison.

29. Suppose I break one of the laws described in answers 22-26. What kind of penalties will I be facing?

The law says "imprisonment for not more than 10 years or a fine of not more than $100,000.00, or both." [21]

30. Does that include the drugs that the other people are making?

No. The penalty for having or providing a place, vehicle, chemicals, or equipment to make or prepare drugs is up to 10 years imprisonment or a fine of not more than $100,000.00, or both. If you actually have drugs or other contraband or if you have been committing other crimes, the penalty will increase.

31. Why is the penalty so high for merely giving someone something that they can use to make drugs?

Society, people who do not care so much about acquiring money, is tired of living with the effects of drug abuse. By removing the people from society who contribute to the illegal drug trade, society hopes to have less crime, suffering, and loss.

32. So I'm facing up to 10 years if I give someone something to use in preparing drugs?

Yes, but you should also know that there are at least five things that can significantly increase the sentence to more than 10 years.

1. If you give someone something in the presense of a minor that the person uses to make drugs, the penalty increases to up to "20 years [in prison] or a fine of not more than $100,000.00, or both." [22]

2. If you give someone something that they use to make drugs that involve "the unlawful generation, treatment, storage, or disposal of hazardous waste," the penalty increases to up to "20 years [in prison] or a fine of not more than $100,000.00, or both." [23]

3. If you give someone something that they use to make drugs "within 500 feet of a residence, business establishment, school property, or church or other house of worship," the penalty increases to up to "20 years [in prison] or a fine of not more than $100,000.00, or both." [24]

4. If you give someone something that they use to make drugs and anyone involved in that violation has "possession, placement, or use of a firearm or any other device designed or intended to be used to injure another person," the penalty increases to up to "25 years [in prison] or a fine of not more than $100,000.00, or both." [25]

5. If you give someone something that they use to make methamphetamine (meth) or similar

substances, the penalty increases to up to "20 years [in prison] or a fine of not more than $25,000, or both." [26]

33. That is a lot of time. If I commit several crimes at once, will they be treated as one big crime or several individual crimes?

Drug crimes are usually treated individually. The law says that the crimes we have discussed thus far can be served consecutively. [27] That means you can get a 20 year sentence, a 10 year sentence, and a 25 year sentenceall from a single eventand you will have to serve them, one after the next, until they are exhausted if your judge day decides to sentence you that way. In this example, that would be 55 years.

Chapter 3

Making and Selling Counterfeit Drugs

34. Okay, regular drug manufacturing and sales is extremely dangerous. I understand. But suppose I only deal in substances that act like illegal drugs but they are not actually those drugs; is that illegal?

The law says "a person shall not create, manufacture, deliver, or possess with intent to deliver a counterfeit substance or a controlled substance analogue intended for human consumption." [28]

35. What does that mean?

It means that virtually any attempt that you might make to sell something that other people think they can use to get intoxicated is illegal.

36. How much prison time would be involved?

The counterfeit substances that might be described by a drug dealer as the same as or similar to cocaine, heroin, or meth are "punishable by imprisonment for not more than 10 years or a fine of not more than $10,000.00, or both." [29]

Other counterfeit substances are "punishable by imprisonment for not more than 5 years or a fine of not more than $5,000.00, or both." [30]

Substances that are very simlar to schedules 1-3 drugs are against the law too. These substances affect the body similarly to schedule 1-3 drugs, and they are "punishable by imprisonment for not more than 15 years or a fine of not more than $250,000.00, or both." [31]

37. So how does this work?

If you create, manufacture, deliver, or possess any substance for the purpose of getting other people to consume it under the belief that it is a "hard" drug, you are committing a serious crime that could send you to prison for up to 10 years and/or receive a $10,000.00 fine.

If you create, manufacture, deliver, or possess any substance that is similar to a drug that is on one of the first three schedules, you could be sent to prison for up to 15 years and/or receive a $250,000.00 fine.

Chapter 4

Possessing Drugs

38. A friend of mine sells drugs, and she told me mere possession of drugs is a misdemeanor. Is that true?

No. The law is clear on this: "A person shall not knowingly or intentionally possess a controlled substance, a controlled substance analogue, or a prescription form unless [they were supplied by a doctor]." [32] From there the law goes on to say that anyone who possess 1,000 or more grams of schedule 1 or 2 narcotic drug or coca-based drug or those kinds of drugs including any mixtures that contain those substances are "guilty of a felony punishable by imprisonment for life or any term of years or a fine of not more than 1,000,000.00, or both." [33]

39. Isn't that the same punishment as it would be if I was selling 1,000 grams?

Yes.

40. But selling drugs and merely having drugs are two different things.

The law does not treat the punishments differently until the amount of drugs is below 50 grams. Think about it this way: If you get caught selling or simply possessing 50 grams of heroin or cocaine, you will be facing up to 20 years in prison and/or a $25,000.00 fine. [34] However, if you get caught selling less than 50 grams of those drugs, you will still be facing a 20 year prison sentence. But if you get caught possessing less than 50 grams of those drugs, you will be facing not more than 4 years of imprisonment and/or up to a $25,000.00 fine. [35]

41. What if I have 99 grams of dry milk mixed with 1 gram of heroin or cocaine?

According to the law, you would be in possession of a 100 gram mixture of schedule 1 or 2 drug, and you would be facing up to 20 years in prison and/or a $250,000.00 fine. [36]

42. Do the same laws apply for methamphetamines?

No. For methamphetamines, possession of any amount is punishable by up to 10 years in prison and/or a fine of up to $15,000.00. [37] However, quantities over a very small amount will almost always be treated as an attempt to manufacture, create, or deliver, rather than to "merely" possess; which means the punishment changes from being up to 10 years, to being up to 20 years. [38]

43. How much jail or prison time does the law designate for possession of drugs that are not related to cocaine, heroin, or methamphetamines?

In genuine cases of pure possession (i.e., no intent to give, sell, or transport the drugs), the law states that possession is "a felony punishable by imprisonment for not more than 2 years or a fine of not more than $2,000.00, or both applies." [39] For marihuana, lysergic acid diethylamide, peyote, mescaline, and a few other drugs, and schedule 5 drugs the punishment and offense status is lowered to a misdemeanor and "imprisonment for not more than 1 year or a fine of not more than $2,000.00, or both." [40]

44. What are some of the dangers that the law does not seem to be mentioning in the answer above?

Drug dealers often try to use the "mere possession" defense to avoid large prison sentences, so judges and juries are often skeptical of people who try to use it even when it is true. People who possess drugs also make themselves a target for robbery. The worst danger though is hidden and slowly develops as the presence of drugs in one's life results in a series of related crimes that involve incarceration, family strife, troubles at school and work, difficulty maintaining relationships, health problems, poor parenting habits, risk to one's children and family, inability to get a good job, financial instability, being ineligible for government jobs (e.g., soldier, police officer, politician) and not being able to own or carry a firearm. The losses that one sustains as a convicted criminal get worse with time if that person is able to avoid the many extreme disasters that often plague the drug community.

APPENDIX

CONTROLLED SUBSTANCES

Schedules 1-5

Drugs are organized into categories called schedules. Schedule 1 drugs are the most dangerous, and schedule 5 drugs are the least dangerous. Below you will find examples of the drugs in each schedule, as well as the criteria used for classifying a drug to a given schedule.

Schedule 1: According to MCLS 333.7211, the authorities "shall place a substance in schedule1 if it finds that the substance has high potential for abuse and has no accepted medical use in treatment in the United States or lacks accepted safety for use in treatment under medical supervision."

According to MCLS 333.7212, examples of schedule1 substances include, but are not limited to, "opiates, including their isomers, esters, the ethers, salts," and related substances including opium derivatives, "materials, compounds, mixtures"...such as Methcathinone, Cat, Ephedrone, the various forms of methamphetamine, lysergic acid disthylamide, marihuana, mescaline, peyote, PCP, Ecstacy, MDMA.

Schedule 2: According to MCLS 333.7213, the authorities "shall place a substance in schedule 2 if it finds all of the following: (a) The substance has high potential for abuse. (b) The substance has currently accepted medical use in treatment in the United States, or currently accepted medical use with severe restrictions. (c) The abuse of the substance may lead to severe pysycic or physical dependence."

According to MCLS 333.7214, examples of schedule 2 substances when not listed in other schedules include, but are not limited to, certain opium and opiate substances, coca leaves and related substances, amphetamine and related substances, marihuana, and related substances.

Schedule 3: According to MCLS 333.7215, the authorities "shall place a substance in schedule 3 if it finds all of the following: (a) The substance has a potential for abuse less than the substances listed in schedules 1 and 2. (b) The substance has currently accepted medical use in treatment in the United States. (c) Abuse of the substance may lead to moderate or low physical dependence or high psychological dependence."

According to MCLS 333.7216, examples of schedule 3 substances include, but are not limited to, Nalorphine, "any substance that contains any quantity of a derivative of barbituric acid," amobarbital, or ketamine.

Schedule 4: According to MCLS 333.7217, the authorities "shall place a substance in schedule 4 if it finds all of the following: (a) The substance has a low potential for abuse relative to substances in schedule 3. (b) The substance has currently accepted medical use in treatment in the United States. (c) Abuse of the substance may lead to limited physical dependence or psychological dependence relative to the substances in schedule 3."

According to MCLS 333.7218, examples of schedule 4 substances include, but are not limited to, Diethylpropion, Phentermine, Pemoline, and Cathine.

Schedule 5: According to MCLS 333.7219, the authorities "shall place a substance in schedule 5 if it finds all of the following: (a) The substance has low potential for abuse relative to the controlled substances listed in schedule 4. (b) The substance has currently accepted medical use in treatment in the United States. (c) The substance has limited physical dependence or psychological dependence liability relative to the controlled substances listed in schedule 4 or the incidence of abuse is such that the substance should be dispensed by a practitioner."

According to MCLS 333.7220, examples of schedule 5 substances include, but are not limited to, any variation of the ingredients in Loperamide and any of various compounds, mixtures, or preperations of other substances with specific regulations on the amount of their active ingredients (e.g., Not more than 200 milligrams of codeine).

NOTES

1. MCLS 333.7401 (1) This is the Michigan law at the date of this publication.

2. MCLS 333.7401 (2)(a)(i)

3. MCLS 333.7401 (2)(a)(ii)

4. MCLS 333.7401 (2)(a)(iii)

5. MCLS 333.7401 (2)(a)(iv)

6. MCLS 333.7401 (2)(b)(ii)

7. MCLS 333.7401 (2)(d)(i)

8. MCLS 333.7401 (2)(d)(ii)

9. MCLS 333.7401 (2)(d)(iii)

10. MCLS 333.7401 (2)(d)

11. 21 USCS 801

12. United States v. Duval, 865 F. Supp. 2d 803 (as cited in 24 M.L.P. 2d Public Health and Welfare 173, p. 14)

13. MCLS 333.7401 (2)(c)

14. MCLS 333.7401 (2)(e)

15. MCLS 333.7217

16. MCLS 333.7219

17. MCLS 333.7401 (2)(f)

18. MCLS 333.7401c (1)(a)

19. MCLS 333.7401c (1)(b)

20. MCLS 333.7401c (1)(c)

21. MCLS 333.7401c (2)(a)

22. MCLS 333.7401c (2)(b)

23. MCLS 333.7401c (2)(c)

24. MCLS 333.7401c (2)(d)

25. MCLS 333.7401c (2)(e)

26. MCLS 333.7401c (2)(f). See also MCLS 333.7214 (c)(ii)

27. MCLS 333.7401c (5)

28. MCLS 333.7402 (1)

29. MCLS 333.7402 (2)(a)

30. MCLS 333.7402 (2)(b)

31. MCLS 333.7402 (2)(e)

32. MCLS 333.7403 (1)

33. MCLS 333.7403 (2)(a)(i)

34. MCLS 333.7401 (2)(a)(iii) and MCLS 333.7403 (2)(a)(iii)

35. MCLS 333.7401 (2)(a)(iv) and MCLS 333.7403 (2)(a)(iv-v)

36. MCLS 333.7403 (2)(a)(iii)

37. MCLS 333.740 (2)(b)(i)

38. MCLS 333.7401 (2)(b)(i)

39. MCLS 333.7403 (2)(b)(ii)

40. MCLS 333.7403 (2)(b-c)

INDEX

Index numbers refer to question numbers, not to page numbers.

AA/NA: 21

acid, peyote, mescaline: 43

arrest: 2

business establishment: 32

chemicals: 24, 26, 27

church: 32

cocaine: 36, 40, 43

common sense: 26

compliance with state law: 17

consecutive sentence: 33

counterfeit prescription form: 3, 19 (See also "prescription form.")

discretion: 26

drugs:

--abuse: 21, 31

--coca-based: 38

--controlled substance: 3, 10, 11, 18, 19, 22, 24, 36, 38, 41, 43

--counterfeit substance: 22, 24, 26, 34, 36

--dealers: 17, 36, 44

--delivering: 3, 4, 34, 37, 42, 43

--habit: 20

--"hard": 12, 37

--hotlines: 21

--illegal industry: 20, 21, 31

--manufacturing, creating, making: 3, 4, 20, 22-24, 26, 27, 30-32, 34, 37, 42

--possessing: 3, 4, 17, 34, 37, 38, 42, 43

--possessing less than 50 grams: 40

--related crimes: 11

--selling: 3, 11, 20, 23, 38, 43

--selling less than 50 grams: 40

--substance analogue: 22, 24, 26, 34, 38

--to be popular: 20

--to make money: 20

Federal Controlled Substances Act: 17

felony: 16, 19, 38, 43

firearms: 32

hazardous waste: 32

heroin: 5, 12, 36, 40, 43

hidden dangers: 44

house of worship: 32

ignorance of law: 17

intent: 3, 34, 43

judicial discretion: 11

juvenile facility: 2

lab equipment: 24, 26, 27

lifestyle: 20

"light" sentence: 11

marijuana/marihuana:

--claiming ignorance: 17, 22

--edibles: 13

--five patients: 17

--growing: 12, 15

--huge fine: 12

--license: 17

--manufacturing and distributing: 17

--medical: 17

--Michigan Medical Marihuana Act: 17

--mixtures: 12

--personal use: 17

--plants: 13, 14

--"practically legal now": 16

--preparation of: 16

--products: 15

--profits from selling: 12

mentor: 21

"mere possession" defense: 44

methamphetamines (meth): 5, 32, 36, 42, 43

minister: 21

minors: 32

mixtures of schedule 1 or 2 drugs: 38, 40

money problems: 21

narcotics: 5, 10, 38

potential for abuse: 18

prescription forms: 3, 19, 38 (See also "counterfeit prescription form.")

residence: 32

schedules (for controlled substances):

--1: 5, 10, 36, 38, 41

--2: 5, 10, 36, 38, 41

--3: 10, 36

--4: 18

--5: 18

school counselor: 21

school property: 32

"that isn't fair": 28

violating federal law: 17

4.

Firearms and Other Weapons

Chapter 1 Selling, Manufacturing, and Distributing Weapons 95

Chapter 2 Altering Weapons 103

Chapter 3 Carrying and Possessing Weapons .. 105

Chapter 4 Aiming and Discharging Weapons .. 111

Notes 117

Index 120

Chapter 1

Selling, Manufacturing, and Distributing Weapons

1. If a person sells a firearm without complying with the laws for doing so, can they go to jail for it?

Yes. The punishment, however, changes depending on the nature of the offense. For instance, selling a firearm that is "'26 inches in length to a person under 18 years of age" is a misdemeanor that is "punishable by imprisonment for not more than 90 days, or a fine of not more than $500.00, or both." [1] The offense becomes a felony if it occurs again, and the punishment is then increased to "imprisonment for not more than 4 years, or a fine of not more than $2,000.00, or both." [2]

2. So the most someone can get for selling a gun is 4 years?

No, that is way off. A variety of laws apply to selling firearms, so the circumstances of the sale determine which law and punishment applies. For example, suppose you meet a person who you learn is running from the law for a crime that carries more than 4 years in prison, which could be a small drug offense or a theft or an assault or any number of other crimes. If you sell that person a firearm, you will be guilty of a felony that carries a punishment of "imprisonment for not more than 10 years, or [] a fine of not more than $5,000,00, or both." [3]

3. So the most I can face is 10 years?

No. Depending on the laws you violate when making the sale, you might face any amount of time. The point here is that several laws govern the selling of firearms, and they carry a wide range of punishments.

4. How much prison time can I get for having a fully-automatic rifle?

The law states: "A person shall not manufacture, sell, offer for sale, or possess any of the following: (a) A machine gun, (b) a muffler or silencer, (c) A bomb or bombshell" and other items. [4] Violations of that law are punishable by imprisonment for not more than 5 years, or a fine of not more than $2,500.00, or both." [5]

5. What is an example of one of the other items listed, besides a machine gun, silencer, and bomb?

A bludgeon, which is a short stick that is larger on one end than the other, often weighted, and commonly used as a weapon. [6] A bludgeon could easily be overlooked in modern society, where guns and knives and devices that use electricity or chemicals are more readily recognized as dangerous weapons, but a bludgeon is nevertheless highly illegal and can result in as much as a 5 year prison sentence. A few more examples of illegal weapons that carry up to a 5 year sentence are blackjacks, metal knuckles, and devices that spray a substance that can disable someone. [7] For the sake of clarity, the last item listed does not include legal self-defense spray or foam devices. [8]

6. A friend of mine has a club that is used to hit fish. Is that illegal too?

No. A "fish billy" is legal if it is purchased and/or used for legal fishing practices. However, walking through neighborhoods with a fish billy, far from a lake or stream, without a fishing pole and tackle box would probably result in the fish billy being seen as a plain old billywhich is another illegal weapon that carries up to 5 years in prison for anyone who manufactures, sells, or possess it. [9]

7. If I was just honestly walking through a neighborhood to go and get my fishing pole, merely having the fish billy wouldn't be illegal though?

That is something you might have to prove to a jury. Some people get their thrills by challenging authority and seeing whether they can prove the "system" wrong or become a martyr for a given cause. If carrying a fish billy is important to you, at least you now know that doing so can result in you facing prosecution and a 5 year prison sentence. The law is clear enough for most people to understand and follow it: however, some people either ignore or do not know it. For instance, one Mr. Norris took a blackjack from one of his customers and planned to return it before the customer left the establishment, but Mr. Norris was arrested first. For what? For possession of the blackjack. The law does not permit possession "for a little while." [10]

8. Can you really get prison time for some types of ammunition?

Yes. By law, manufacturing, distributing, selling, or using armor Piercing ammunition is illegal and is "punishable by imprisonment for not more than 4 years, or a fine of not more than $2,000.00, or both." [11]

9. How can you know if your ammo is armor piercing?

The "projectile or projectile core" will be constructed "of tungsten alloys, steel, iron, brass, bronze, beryllium copper," or a combination of these, and it will be able to be fired from a pistol. [12] Although the distinction between some of these substances may be difficult to make, legally purchasing standard ammunition from licensed dealers is very easy. Problems often arise when people purchase illegal ammunition or attempt to manufacture illegal ammunition. A single round can easily be lost, only to resurface later during a police officer's search of one's car or garage or property.

10. I want to buy a semi-automatic firearm and convert it into a fully automatic firearm; is that illegal?

Yes. Besides the crime of owning a fully automatic weapon, you will also be committing a crime by manufacturing, selling, distributing, or possessing a device to convert a semiautomatic firearm. This crime is "punishable by imprisonment for not more than 4 years, or a fine of not more than $2,000.00, or both." [13] Even showing someone else how to make or install a conversion device is punishable by up to 4 years in prison. [14] With so much dangerous information available, this law can easily be regarded as outdated and dismissed because it seems like "everyone" is showing people how to do illegal things; however, the law is applied to each person individually. That means one person may get away with breaking it several times while another person gets caught and sent to prison after the first offense.

11. A friend of mine is trying to make switchblades because they are rare and he thinks he can make money selling them. Is there a law against that?

Unlawful sale or possession of a pocket knife opened by mechanical device is a misdemeanor punishable by up to 1 year in prison and/or a $300.00 fine. [15] Making or converting a knife to open automatically by a switch on the handle or by pressure on it or by any other mechanical means makes the sale and possession of the knife illegal, but the law does not necessarily end here: if your friend puts a switchblade in his pocket and goes out into the public, he will be guilty of a much more serious crime called carrying concealed weapon, which we will discuss in chapter 3.

12. I'm thinking about buying a bunch of guns that a guy stole and selling them individually. If I get caught selling a stolen gun, how much time can I get?

You will be facing up to 10 years for a stolen firearm or stolen ammunition that you "receive, conceal, store, barter, sell, dispose of, pledge, or accept as security for a loan." [16] This is a serious crime that occurs as soon as you accept possession of the stolen firearms or ammunition. Each separate sale that you make can result in up to another 10-year sentence being stacked on top of another. The actions themselves, buying and selling some stolen guns, might not seem like a big deal, but they become a big deal when the charges, trials, and prison sentences start adding up.

13. Suppose I just move some stolen guns from one place to another, is that a crime?

Yes. The law actually says that "a person who transports or ships a stolen firearm or ammunition" is guilty of a felony that has the same sentence (i.e., up to 10 years in prison) that selling stolen firearms carries. [17] This means the driver and everyone else who is involved in the sale of stolen firearms will face prison time. Stolen firearms are contributing to the shooting and killing of countless innocent men, women, and children. People who have stolen firearms often feel less responsible for how they use them because the firearms are not actually theirs; so selling and transporting stolen guns is contributing to the crimes that later occur with those weapons.

CHAPTER 2

ALTERING WEAPONS

14. I want to make a "sawed-off" shotgun, but I don't know how long to make the barrel. Is there a law on barrel length?

Barrels cannot be cut down to 26 inches or less without complying with designated legislation (i.e., section 2 or 2a of 1927 PA 372, MCL 28.422 and 28.422a). Making, manufacturing, transferring, or possessing "a short-barreled shotgun or a short-barreled rifle" is punishable by up to 5 years in prison or a fine of not more than $2,500.00, or both. [18] Therefore, the barrel has to be over 26 inches or you will have to seek further information on how to proceed.

15. If I scratch out or change the serial number on a gun, is that illegal?

Yes. Altering, removing, or changing any of the identifying information on a firearm is a felony that is punishable by up to 2 years in prison or a fine of up to $1,000.00, or both. And any firearm found in this damaged state will be treated as evidence that the person in possession of it is responsible for the damage. [19]

Some crimes rely heavily on the jury to decide whether the defendant had the intent to do certain actions that are illegal. This is not one of those crimes: if you are found in the possession of a weapon that has the identification markings damaged, the court presumes that you did it, which is punishable by up to 2 years in prison.

16. What else might happen if I get caught with a gun that has no serial numbers?

Your house, car, and property might be searched to see whether you have anything else that ties you to other crimes; you might get charged with any unsolved crimes that are linked to that weapon; you will almost certainly be found guilty of a felony because possession is very easy to establish; you will be ineligible for a permit to carry a pistol; you will not be able to get a job in security or law enforcement or several other vocations, the military will not accept you; and the felony on your record will put you at a greater risk of being sentenced to larger amounts of time if you get convicted of another crime in the future. Many other losses occur when you become a felon, but these are some of them.

CHAPTER 3

CARRYING AND POSSESSING WEAPONS

17. Where can a person legally possess a weapon?

The short answer is (1) at home, (2) at one's place of business, and (3) on other land one possesses.[20] The law becomes more complicated after that. This law actually applies to dangerous weapons such as "a dagger, dirk, stiletto, double-edged nonfolding stabbing instrument of any length, or other dangerous weapon, except a hunting knife adapted and carried as such."[21]

18. Where can a person legally possess pistols?

Same as above. The law specifically states however that "A person shall not carry a pistol concealed on or about his or her person" or in a vehicle, without a license to do so.[22] The penalty for carrying a concealed weapon is imprisonment for not more than 5 years or up to a n$2,500.00 fine.[23]

19. If in carry a knife, a "hunting knife," will I be breaking the law?

Tryijgntonfind exceptions to law is an imprecise practice; what one person is able to getaway with anther person might be sent to prison for doing. I suspect people carry hunting knives, but the law says doing so is illegal. For example, Mr. Wright was prosecuted for carrying his hunting knife; however, the knife was not a common hunting knife, he was not wearing hunting clothes, and it was new tnhntingnseason.[24] Simple reasons like that are all it takes to find someone guilty.

20. How strict is the law about carrying pistols?

Extremely strict. You either have a permit to carry or you do not. If you are caught carrying without a permit, there aren't any excuses that will get you out of that felony conviction and sentence.

21. Why don't the legislators want people carrying weapons?

Several cases cite the law being established to "discourage quarrelling [people] from suddenly drawing and using concealed weapons."[25] People, when angry or scared, often tend to do things they later regret. The legislators seem to be attempting to control or prevent some of these things by removing the weapons by removing the weapons from the matter, but there may be other reasons.

22. Is carrying a pistol or other weapon for self-protection a good defense to the charge of carrying concealed weapon?

No. In fact, it is a terrible defense. The law does not all own for such carrying without a permit.[26]

23. What is the purpose of down ng a pistol if I can't carry it?

In People v. Clark the purpose of down ng a pistol is "to allow persons to defend those areas [one's dwelling house or place of business or other owned lands.]"[27] The law supports these purposes by explicitly identifying the areas in which one may lawfully posses a pistol and other such dangerous weapons.[28]

24. If I am in a car with a bunch of people and the authorities find a pistol in he car, can I get in trouble?

In People v. Little, the defendant was in a car with several other people and weapons. The defendant "was not shown to have actual physical possession of the weapons," but he was convicted due to his associations with he others. In other words, he was not a stranger who suddenly found himself in the midst of people with weapons: he was among people he knew, and he got convicted with them.[29] The same could happen to anyone else.

25. Is it illegal to pull a knife or gun on someone?

Carrying a firearm or dangerous weapon with unlawful intent sounds very.Mich like what you are describing. This law prohibits oneself and going about in society with the purpose of illegally using weapons against another person. [30] The punishment for violating this law is imprisonment for up to 5 years or a fine of up to $2,500.00. [31] In this crime you do not actual make contact with another person.

26. Would a BB gun count?

Smooth-bore BB guns that shoot BB's of not greater than .177 caliber are not considered a firearm, and the Legislator has determined that BB guns of this sort do not qualify as a "dangerous or deadly weapon." [32] However, taking a BB gun to confront someone is extremely dangerous for many other reasons: the other person could think the BB gun is a rifle and arm themselves nor call someone elsepossibly the policeand the matter could quickly spin out of control. People have been shot and killed for carrying less threatening items to a confrontation.

27. What does felony firearm mean?

It is a reference to the law against carrying or possessing a firearm when committing or attempting to commit a felony. If you have a firearm in your possession while committing or attempting to commit a felony you automatically get this felony added on top of the one(s) you are committing or attempting. The first felony firearm conviction is punishable by a mandatory 2-year prison sentence. The next felony firearm offence is punishable by a mandatory 5-year prison sentence; additional felony firearm offences, 10-years each. [33]

This law is special for a number of reasons: (1) the sentences are mandatory, which means the judge does not have the discretion to give less than 2, 5, or 10 years, depending on the previous number of felony firearm offences one has been convicted of; (2) the felon firearm sentence is stacked on top of any other sentence that one might receive, which means a 4-year felony could turn into a 9-year felony or a 14-year if it occurs with a 2nd or 3rd felony firearm; and (3) a felony firearm sentence is not eligible for any sentence reductions or parole, which means every single day of the sentence has to be served before the person can be released from custody—no exceptions. [34, 35, 36] Another interesting characteristic of this law is that it includes BB guns, which are generally excluded from laws that send people to prison. [37]

28. Why is the punishment for felony firearm more harsh than for most other crimes?

The legislature seems to be trying to deter people, from using firearms during crimes, by increasing the amount of time that a given offense carries, just by virtue of the presence of a firearm.

29. Suppose someone has a gun but it does not work or have any bullets, can they still get a felony-firearm?

Yes. Operability is not even discussed at trial. The law is only concerned with whether a firearm was present during the commission or attempted commission of the felony. [38] The firearm can be empty of bullets or even broken, and having it during any part of the commission of a felony automatically adds felony-firearm to the charges that will be faced.

Chapter 4

Aiming and Discharging Weapons

30. If a person is at home and is legally in possession of an unloaded firearm, is it illegal for that person to point the unloaded firearm at another person?

Yes. Whether the firearm is loaded or unloaded does not matter. The law says: "A person who intentionally but without malice [the intent to commit a wrongful act that will result in harm to another] points or aims a firearm at or toward another person is guilty of a misdemeanor punishable by imprisonment for not more than 93 days or a fine of not more than $500.00, or both. [39] Note here that no one has to get injured. The firearm does not even have to discharge. The crime occurs as soon as the end of the barrel is pointed toward another person. You don't have to wish the other person harm or anything else; the pointing of the weapon at someone else is the crime.

31. What if the gun discharges but you didn't mean for it to?

If the firearm is pointed at or toward another without malice and the firearm discharges but does not injure anyone, the person in possession of the firearm "is guilty of a misdemeanor punishable by imprisonment for" up to 1 year or a fine of up to $500.00, or both. [40]

32. Does the law say anything about firing a firearm from an automobile?

Intentionally discharging a firearm from a motorized vehicle is definitely a serious crime; how serious, however, depends on the circumstances. The punishment for violations of this law are divided into four categories:

"(a) If the violation endangers the safety of another individual," the penalty is imprisonment for up to 10 years and/or a $15,000.00 fine.

"(b) If the violation causes any physical injury to another individual," the penalty is imprisonment for up to 15 years and/or a $15,000.00 fine.

"(c) If the violation causes the serious impairment of a body function of another individual," the penalty is imprisonment for up to 20 years and/or a $25,000.00 fine.

"(d) If the violation causes the death of another individual," the penalty is imprisonment for life or any number of years. [41]

33. Do these sentences get stacked on top of any other crimes that a person might also be convicted of?

Yes. The sentence for intentionally discharging a firearm from a motor vehicle must be served separately from any other sentences that might also apply. [42] This is probably so people will avoid firing weapons from automobiles. The large amount of prison time that this crime carries can be a good deterrent for people who wish to remain free.

34. Suppose a person in an automobile shoots at a house, does that make it worse than the crime of discharging a firearm from a vehicle at something else?

Discharging a firearm from a motor vehicle is a separate crime from discharging a firearm at a dwelling or potentially occupied structure. Shooting, even once, at a house or other structure that might have someone inside of it carries the same penalties as discharging a firearm from a motor vehicle (See answer to question 32). [43]

35. Does that mean that once I shoot from a vehicle that it doesn't matter what I shoot at because the prison sentence will be the same?

No. That is not what it means. Think of it like this: firing a shot at a house from a car is two separate crimes: (1) firing at a house and (2) firing from a vehicle. If no one is hit, you will be facing up to 10 years in prison for each offense; if someone is hit but not very seriously, you will be facing up to 15 years in prison for each offense; and the possible sentences go on from there, getting progressively worse as the harm to the victims gets worse. However, the fact that you can get 20 years for shooting at a house should tell you how serious the courts are treating this crime.

36. If I shoot at a garage, does that count?

Yes. A garage, a shed, a tent, an apartment, a trailer, a condominium, a barn, a workshop, a store, a restaurant, a bar, a club, or any other "potentially occupied structure" counts. Imagine getting incarcerated for even 5 years for shooting at an empty building.

37. The building can be empty?

Yes. The law that we are discussing is against shooting at a structure, not at a person; therefore, whether it is occupied or empty is irrelevant.

38. If I shoot over the structure or at the dirt in front of it, does that count?

Yes. The word "at" includes everything "in the direction of" a structure. [44] You don't have to hit anyone or even the structure itself. The point of this law is to discourage people from shooting at anything that might have a person inside of it

Notes

1. MCLS 750.223 (1)

2. MCLS 750.223 (2)

3. MCLS 750.223 (4)

4. MCLS 750.224 (1)

5. MCLS 750.224 (2)

6. People v. Beasley, 198 Mich. App. 40, 1993 Mich. App. LEXIS 23 (Mich. Ct. App. 1993).

7. MCLS 750.224 (1)(d-e)

8. MCLS 750.224 (3)(a)

9. People v. Battles, 109 Mich. App. 384, 1981 Mich. App. LEXIS 3278 (Mich. Ct. App. 1981), and see supra note 7.

10. People v. Norris, 40 Mich. App. 45, 1972 Mich. App. LEXIS 1184 (Mich. Ct. App. 1972).

11. MCLS 750.224c (1)

12. MCLS 750.224c (3)(a)

13. MCLS 750.224e (1-2)

14. MCLS 750.224e (1)(b)

15. MCLS 750.226a

16. MCLS 750.535b (2)

17. MCLS 750.535b (1)

18. MCLS 750.224b (1-4)

19. MCLS 750.230

20. MCLS 750.227 (1)

21. id.

22. MCLS 750.227 (2)

23. MCLS 750.227 (3)

24. People v. Wright, 97 Mich. App. 411, 1980 Mich. App. LEXIS 2669 (Mich. Ct. App. 1980).

25. People v. Adams, 173 Mich. App. 60, 1988 Mich. App. LEXIS 681 (Mich. Ct. App. 1988); People v. Coffey, 153 Mich. App. 311, 1986 Mich. App. LEXIS 2767 (Mich. Ct. App. 1986); People v. Emery, 150 Mich. App. 657, 1986 Mich. App. LEXIS 2547 (Mich. Ct. App. 1986).

26. People v. Townsel, 13 Mich. App. 600, 1968 Mich. App. LEXIS 1109 (Mich. Ct. App. 1968).

27. People v. Clark, 21 Mich. App. 712, 1970 Mich. App. LEXIS 2143 (Mich. Ct. App. 1970).

28. See supra notes 20 and 22.

29. People v. Little, 58, Mich. App. 12, 1975 Mich. App. LEXIS 1660 (Mich. Ct. App. 1975).

30. MCLS 750.226 (1)

31. MCLS 750.226 (2)

32. People v. Ackah-Essien, 311 Mich. App. 13, 2015 Mich. App. LEXIS 1155 (Mich. Ct. App. 2015).

33. MCLS 750.227b (1-3)

34. MCLS 750.227b (1)

35. MCLS 750.227b (3)

36. MCLS 750.227b (4)

37. MCLS 750.227b (2)

38. People v. Thompson, 189 Mich. App. 85, 1991 Mich. App. LEXIS 171 (Mich. Ct. App. 1991).

39. MCLS 750.233 (1)

40. MCLS 750.234 (1)

41. MCLS 750.234a (1)(a-d)

42. MCLS 750.234a (4)

43. MCLS 750.234b (1)

44. People v. Wilson, 230 Mich. App. 590, 1998 Mich. App. LEXIS 193 (Mich. Ct. App. 1998).

INDEX

Index numbers refer to question numbers, not to page numbers.

armor piercing ammunition: 8, 9

blackjack: 5, 7

bomb: 4, 5

carrying concealed weapon: 11, 18, 20-22

consecutive sentence: 12

dangerous weapon: 23-26

firearm:

--aiming at someone: 25, 30

--automatic: 4, 10

--BB gun: 26

--broken: 29

--conversion device: 10

--discharging: 31

--discharging at dwelling/poss. occupied structure: 34-38

--discharging from a motor vehicle: 32-35

--distribute: 8, 10

--felony: 27, 29

--machine gun: 4, 5

--manufacture: 4, 8-10, 14
--offer for sale: 4
--permit to carry: 16, 20
--possession: 4, 7, 10, 12, 14-15, 17-18, 24, 27
--"sawed-off" shotgun: 14
--selling: 1-4, 8, 10, 12, 13
--semiautomatic: 10
--serial number: 15, 16
--stolen: 12, 13
--transferring: 14
"hunting knife": 19
intent: 15, 25
knife: 17
law enforcement: 16
metal knuckles: 5
military: 16
running from the law: 2
self-protection: 22
serial numbers: 15, 16
silencer/muffler: 4, 5
stolen ammunition: 12
switchblade:

--possession: 11

--selling: 11

transporting stolen firearms or ammunition: 13

5.

Homicide

Chapter 1 First Degree Murder 125

Chapter 2 Second Degree Murder 131

Chapter 3 Manslaughter 135

Chapter 4 Related Homicide Laws 137

Notes 141

Index 143

Chapter 1

First Degree Murder

1. What is first degree murder?

First degree murder is the worst form of murder because it involves the "willful, deliberate, and premeditated killing" of another person. [1] This means the offender has wanted someone to die and has taken specific, calculated steps to bring about that person's death. In the wording of the law, reference to poisoning someone or "lying in wait," which means ambushing someone, is made. These are examples of how first degree murder might be carried out; however, many such examples could be given. Virtually any attempt to kill someone that involves thinking about it ahead of time is first degree murder.

Michigan does not use the death penalty anymore to punish offenders who are convicted of first degree murder. Instead, violators are imprisoned "for life without eligibility for parole." [2] This means the people who go to prison for first degree murder stay in prison until they die. For one person that might be just a few more years while for another person that might be 50 or more years. Regardless of how long a person who is sentenced to life without eligibility for parole serves, the parole board has no authority to release him or her. Unlike the Hollywood version of criminal justice, sentences of life in prison actually mean that in Michigan.

2. Suppose I am committing a crime and someone dies in the process, but I did not kill them. Is that manslaughter?

No. What you are describing is called felony murder. It is a controversial piece of law that makes any one of a long list of crimes that result in death automatically punishable by life without eligibility for parole in prison. The law actually says that a person who commits "murder [ ] in the perpetration of, or attempt to perpetrate, arson, [rape], child abuse [ ], a major [drug] offense, robbery, carjacking, breaking and entering [ ], home invasion [ ], larceny of any kind, extortion, kidnapping," or a number of other crimes is guilty of felony murder. [3]

3. What does that mean?

It means you will be facing life in prison if someone dies as a result of you committing or trying to commit a crime against them.

4. So if someone runs out into traffic and gets hit by a bus while trying to avoid me robbing them, I will get life in prison for murder?

Yes. That is exactly how the felony murder law works. If anyone dies as a result of your crime or attempted crime, you will be held responsible for their death.

5. That's not fair. Just because I commit a crime does not mean that I am trying to kill anyone.

Think about it this way: when you commit a crime against someone, they are innocent. That means you are starting the unfairness. If they die because you unfairly committed a crime against them, you have to accept responsibility for that death even though you did not mean for them to die. You wished them I'll, and they got what you wished upon them and more. It's your fault.

6. So if I break into a house and someone in there falls down the stairs and dies, I will get life in prison?

Yes. The home invasion is the felony that turns the death into murder. In other words, the person is dead because you broke into his or her house.

7. And if I go to a house to buy drugs and someone gets killed?

There are some exceptions, but depending on the circumstances, you could easily wind up charged with felony murder.

8. What does "larceny of any kind" mean in the answer to #2 above?

It means you will face life in prison for felony murder if anyone dies, for any reason, when you steal from them.

9. Will I get charged with murder if someone dies when I try to steal just one penny from them?

The penny is irrelevant. You will be charged with murder because while trying to steal from someone you created a situation that resulted in their death.

10. This just does not make sense to me. How can I be charged with murder if I don't want anyone to die?

Suppose you let someone borrow your phone and it gets damaged because they dropped it. Does it make sense to you that they did not mean for your phone to get damaged? Of course it does. You can easily understand how someone can accidentally break your phone. You can also have a reasonable expectation that they will pay for the damages.

Now suppose someone takes your phone without permission and breaks it on accident. At this point do you really care whether they broke it on purpose or on accident? No, all you really care about is getting your phone back in good working order. The felony murder law is similar to that except it is not about broken property; it is about destroyed lives. If you commit certain crimes and someone dies, by law, you are responsible for the death. This is just like if you steal property and accidentally break it. Regardless of your intent, you are responsible for the broken property.

Chapter 2

Second Degree Murder

11. What is second degree murder?

"Second degree murderall other kinds of murder shall be murder of the second degree, and shall be punished by imprisonment in the state prison for life, or any term of years, in the discretion of the court trying the same." [4] That is second degree murder.

12. What does that mean?

It means Michigan has two forms of murder: first degree murder, which is the premeditated kind, and second degree murder, which is all other kinds.

13. What is felony murder, first or second degree?

Felony murder is a form of first degree. When you commit one of the crimes discussed in the answer to question 2, you automatically assume responsibility for the lives of all parties involved. That means that you are responsible if anyone dies during the crime.

14. Will I be given first degree murder if I am drunk or high and kill someone?

If you premeditate a murder—whether or not you are intoxicated—you will be guilty of first degree murder, which is punishable by life in prison without the possibility of parole. Second degree murder is often associated with intoxication because intoxicated people sometimes kill people in a drug or alcohol induced rage. Second degree murders that involve drug or alcohol abuse have the element of malice, a desire to harm or kill, but they do not include premeditation.

15. What exactly does it take to prove second degree murder?

The prosecutor must establish that the defendant intentionally killed or tried to kill or severely bodily injure the victim. If the prosecutor cannot prove that, the prosecutor can still get a conviction by showing that the defendant killed the victim as a result of "a wanton and wilful act the natural tendency of which is to cause death or great bodily harm." [6] This wanton and wilful act can be purposeful or blatantly negligent, which means, for example, the defendant can grab a pistol in an intoxicated rage and murder someone during a confrontation or the intoxicated defendant can disregard speed limits and race into a busy intersection causing car crashes that result in the death of other people. [7] In either case we find examples of second degree murder.

16. What are some more examples?

Shaking a ladder, to scare someone, while they are on the ladder. If they get scared and fall off the ladder and die, you would probably be convicted of second degree murder because shaking a ladder is clearly an intentional act that puts someone in harm's way. Other examples might be punching someone when they are not looking, throwing objects into traffic, hitting someone with a weapon (e.g., a bat).

17. Can I really go to prison if I get into a wreck and someone dies because I was driving too fast?

Yes. If you were clearly going too fast for a given situation, the fault is yours, and second degree murder applies. [8] Malice is an element that has to be established in the second degree trial; however, malice "may be present without actual intent to kill." [9] That means you can do other things that show that you mean harm to other people. An example of malice without actual intent to kill could be driving drunk and dangerously, which endangers other people. Generally, drunk drivers are not known for intentionally killing people; however, because the dangers of drunk driving are so obvious and well known, people who kill people by drunk driving are usually given large prison sentences related to second degree murder or manslaughter.

Chapter 3

Manslaughter

18. What is manslaughter?

Manslaughter is a category of illegal killing that is "punishable by imprisonment in the state prison, not more than 15 years or by fine of not more than $7,500, or both." [10] Notice here should be given to the fact that the manslaughter law can be defined in a few different ways, particularly with reference to the categories of voluntary and involuntary manslaughter. [11] An early and simple definition of manslaughter is "the unlawful killing of another without malice, express[ed] or implied." [12]

19. Earlier you described felony murder, but you never said what a person would face if they committed a misdemeanor and someone died as a result of it. Would it be "misdemeanor murder"?

No. It would be manslaughter. The law is clear: "If, in doing an act which would have been a misdemeanor at common law, a person causes death of another, he is guilty of manslaughter." [13] That means you will be held responsible for your actions, whether they are large or small crimes, if anyone dies from them. Imagine all of the ways that a person could die from relatively minor crimes that you might commit. Could someone die if you burn garbage on your property? Could someone die if you run out into traffic to cross a busy road? Could someone die if you leave dangerous substances like gasoline, bleach, and laundry detergent unattended? These questions are just three of many hundreds of such questions that responsible people face daily. Irresponsible people choose to do things that put themselves and others in danger; however, if someone gets injured or killed, the person who created the dangerous situation will then face very serious criminal charges.

Chapter 4

Related Homicide Laws

20. If I sell or deliver cocaine, heroin, method, or other "hard" drugs and someone dies from them, can I be prosecuted for that?

Yes, absolutely. If you in any illegal manner give someone a schedule 1 or 2 drugother than marihuanaand that person or someone else dies from the drug, you will face a "felony punishable by imprisonment for life or any term of years." [14] This is the equivalent of second degree murder in one sense and felony murder in another sense. People in the drug trade never know when people are going to tell the authorities about their drug dealing; however, when people overdose and die, their friends and family often want the person who gave them the drugs to go to prison. Michigan law supports life sentences or any term of years for drug dealers or people who deliver drugs to people who later overdose on them.

21. How does the law look at someone if they assaults a pregnant woman and the unborn baby dies?

The assault to the mother is obviously a crime; however, the effect that the assault has on the unborn baby is also the responsibility of the assaulter. The law states: "The wilful killing of an unborn [ ] child by any injury to the mother. . .shall be deemed manslaughter." [15]

22. So if I just push a pregnant woman and she falls, I will be guilty of manslaughter?

Yes. But you do not even have to make contact: you could just threaten a pregnant woman. If your threat leads to a miscarriage, you could spend the next 15 years in prison. [16]

23. If I am following all of the laws, can I get found guilty of murder if I hit someone with my car?

If you follow all of the laws, you will help your case for not getting found guilty. Sometimes people accidentally walk out in front of cars, and the tragedy is no fault of the driver. You should, however, understand that negligent homicide, for example, can be applied to someone who hits someone else while obeying the speed limit. if that is hard to imagine, think of it this way: driving 35 miles per hour where that speed is legal but inappropriate for the situation (e.g., in a foggy neighborhood while school children are walking to school) could lead to a manslaughter charge if you hit and kill someone with your car. In other words, "driving at an immoderate speed shall not depend upon the speed fixed by law for operating vehicles." [17] This means that, even if you follow the laws, you can still be held responsible if your actions harm others. As people mature they tend to think about the consequences of their actions more. Avoiding the many situations that might lead to incarceration requires both a willingness to obey the law and a willingness to avoid actions that might end in the injury or death of others.

Notes

1. MCLS 750.316 (1)(a)

2. MCLS 750.316 (1)

3. MCLS 750.316 (1)(b)

4. MCLS 750.317

5. People v. Simmons, 134 Mich. App. 779, 1984 Mich. App. LEXIS 2675 (Mich. Ct. App. 1984).

6. People v. Klave, 130 Mich. App. 388, 1983 Mich. App. LEXIS 3430 (Mich. Ct. App. 1983).

7. People v. Arnett, 239 Mich. 123, 1927 Mich. LEXIS 731 (Mich. 1927) (While resisting arrest, the intoxicated party shoots and fatally wounds officer); People v. Aldrich, 246 Mich. App. 101, 2001 Mich. App. LEXIS 107 (Mich. Ct. App. 2001) (Elements of second degree murder were established in case of street racing into an intersection while intoxicated).

8. People v. Mayhew, 236 Mich. App. 112, 1999 Mich. App. LEXIS 150 (Mich. Ct. App. 1999); People v. Vasquez, 129 Mich. App. 691, 1983 Mich. App. LEXIS 3274 (Mich. Ct. App. 1983).

9. People v. Davis, 76 Mich. App. 187, 1977 Mich. App. LEXIS 901 (Mich. Ct. App. 1977).

10. MCLS 750.321

11. People v. Townes, 391Mich. 578, 1974 Mich. LEXIS 155 (Mich. 1974); People v. Carter, 387 Mich. 397, 1972 LEXIS 172 (Mich. 1972).

12. People v. Droste, 160 Mich. 66, 1910 Mich. LEXIS 729 (Mich. 1910).

13. People v. Brown, 37 Mich. App. 565, 1972 Mich. App. LEXIS 1730 (Mich. Ct. App. 1972).

14. MCLS 750.317a

15. MCLS 750.322

16. Larkin v. Cahalan, 389 Mich. 533.

17. People v. McMurchy, 249 Mich. 147, 1930 Mich. LEXIS 678 (Mich. 1930).

INDEX

Index numbers refer to question numbers, not to page numbers.

ambushing: 1

arson: 1

assault: 21

breaking and entering: 2

burn garbage: 19

buying drugs: 7

carjacking: 2

causing car crashes: 15

child abuse: 2

cocaine: 20

confrontation: 15

death penalty: 1

discretion of the court: 11

disregarding speed limits: 15

driving too fast: 17

drug dealing: 20

drug or alcohol abuse: 14

drug or alcohol induced rage: 14

drug trade: 20

drunk driving: 17

extortion: 2

felony: 6, 20

great bodily harm: 15

"hard" drugs: 20

heroin: 20

hitting someone when they are not looking: 16

hitting someone with a weapon: 16

Hollywood version of criminal justice: 1

home invasion: 2, 6

intent: 10, 17

intoxicated: 14

intoxicated rage: 15

irresponsible people: 33

kidnapping: 2

larceny: 2, 8, 9

life without the possibility of parole: 1-4, 6, 8, 14, 20

lying in wait: 1

major drug offenses: 2

malice (desire to kill or harm): 14, 17, 18

marihuana (marijuana): 20

methamphetamine: 20

miscarriage: 22

misdemeanor: 19

murder:

--felony: 2, 4, 7, 8, 10, 13, 19, 20

--first degree: 1, 12-14

--killing: 1, 5, 7, 14, 17-19, 23

--manslaughter: 17-19, 21-23

--negligent (homicide): 23

--second degree: 11, 12, 14, 16, 17, 20

--voluntary and involuntary manslaughter: 18

--willful, deliberate, and premeditated: 1, 12, 14

negligent: 15

overdose: 20

parole board: 1

poisoning: 1

pregnant women: 21

rape: 2

responsible people: 19

robbery: 2, 4

schedule 1 or 2 drugs: 20

"that's not fair": 5

they are innocent: 5

throwing objects into traffic: 16

unfairness: 5

wanton and willful act: 15, 16

6.

Larceny

Chapter 1 Larceny 149

Chapter 2 Larceny from a Motor Vehicle 153

Chapter 3 Larceny from a Building 157

Chapter 4 Larceny from a Person 163

Chapter 5 Retail Fraud 167

Notes 171

Index 174

CHAPTER 1

LARCENY

1. What is larceny?

Larceny is theft.

2. What does the law say about it?

The law is clear on the subject: A person who steals the money or property of another person is guilt of larceny. [1]

3. Are there different levels of larceny, like first, second, and third degree larceny?

No. The law distinguishes types of larceny such as larceny from a person or larceny from a building, but the levels of larceny are distinguished by the dollar value of the larceny.

4. So the more you steal, the more time you can be given if you get convicted?

Basically, yes. If you steal anything that is worth $20,000,00 or more, you can be sent to prison for up to "10 years or [receive] a fine of not more than $15,000.00 or 3 times the value of the property stolen, whichever is greater, or both imprisonment and a fine." [2]

However, if what you steal "has a value of $1,000.00 or more but less than $20,000.00," you can be sent to prison for up to "5 years or [receive] a fine of not more than $10,000.00 or 3 times the value of the property stolen, whichever is greater, or both imprisonment and a fine." [3]

If what you steal "has a value of less than $1,000.00," you can be "imprisoned for not more than 1year or [be given] a fine of not more than $2,000.00 or 3 times the value of the property stolen, whichever is greater, or both imprisonment and a fine." [4]

Theft of property worth less than $200 is punishable by up to 93 days in jail.

This schedule of theft values and prison sentences applies to several of the larceny laws that will be covered later, so to make it easier to remember, just think $20,000.00+ is up to 10 years in prison; $1,000.00 less than $20,000.00 is up to 5 years in prison; $200 less than $1,000.00 is up to 1 year in prison; and less than $200 is up to 93 days in jail.

5. If my friend steals $500 in cash but I only steal $500 in used car tires, who will face the most time in jail or prison?

You will both be in danger of receiving up to 1 year in jail or prison because the dollar value of what you both stole is $500. In other words, you can steal $500 worth of anything, and the punishment will be the same. In a sense, Michigan law does not use anything other than the dollar value to determine the punishment.

6. So I could steal $1,000.00 in gold and another person could steal $1,000.00 in broken toys, and we would both get up to 5 years in prison?

Yes. That is exactly how it works. The stolen gold might be one tiny bar and the broken toys might fill a warehouse, but when you sell them, you will get $1,000.00 for the gold and $1,000.00 for the broken toys. Therefore, they both have the same dollar value, which means the punishment for stealing them will be the same too. This system makes it easier for judges and prosecutors to determine how bad someone's theft is.

7. Can I get more time in prison or jail if I have a prior conviction for larceny?

Yes. The prosecuting attorney may seek an enhanced sentence, but the details of how much additional time you would be facing due to having a record of larceny would be calculated and discussed by the authorities handling your case.

8. Suppose I stole $500 worth of items each month for a year. Would I face 12 cases of larceny that could get me up to a year in jail or prison each, or would I face 1 case of larceny that could get me up to 5 years in prison?

The law states "The value of property stolen in separate incidents pursuant to a scheme or course of conduct within any 12-month period may be aggregated to determine the total value of the property stolen." [5] This means that by law, all of the thefts over the past year that you have committed against a person or business can be added together and treated as one big crime. The judge has the final say as to whether you will face one big charge or several smaller ones.

Chapter 2

Larceny from a Motor Vehicle

9. Recently I thought about stealing a radio out of a car. If I did that, what could happen to me?

Stealing from automobiles is dangerous because some people will attack you if they catch you breaking into their vehicle or property. Besides that obvious threat, the law holds that it is a felony, "punishable by imprisonment for not more than 5 years or a fine of not more than $10,000.00, or both" to steal or unlawfully remove "any wheel, tire, air bag, catalytic converter, radio, stereo, clock, telephone, computer, or other electronic device in or on any motor vehicle, house trailer, trailer, or semitrailer." [7]

10. So I could get 5 years in prison for stealing anything out of a vehicle?

No. The items listed above have been specifically set apart and given a punishment of up to 5 years in prison regardless of their actual value.

11. So if I steal a broken phone out of a car, I can get up to 5 years in prison?

Yes. The items listed above are named individually because the law makers want the judges to pay special attention to cases that involve them.

12. How much time in jail or prison will I get for stealing something out of a vehicle that is not listed above?

The answer to question #4, above, tells you the punishments that apply to stealing other items from vehicles.

13. So if I steal a $500 coat out of a car, I will face up to 1 year in jail.

Yes.

14. Can the sentence be enhanced if I have prior larceny conviction?

Yes. [8]

15. If I repeatedly steal from cars in a parking lot or neighborhood, will all of those thefts be combined together or be treated individually if I get caught?

That would be up to the judge and your prosecutor to determine (see the answer to question #8 above).

16. Suppose I am stealing from a vehicle something that only costs a few dollars and I damage the vehicle in the process. Will this damage of the vehicle affect the punishment I will face?

Absolutely. Breaking, tearing, cutting, or otherwise damaging "any part of [a] motor vehicle, house trailer, trailer, or semitrailer "while stealing any propertyregardless of the value of the propertyis "a felony punishable by imprisonment for not more than 5 years or a fine of not more than $10,000.00, or both." [9]

17. Does the law say anything about renting or leasing cars and not returning them?

Yes. That is part of the larceny from a vehicle law. It says that anyone who rents or leases a vehicle, trailer, or other tangible physical property and refuses to return it on time is guilty of larceny of a rented motor vehicle, trailer, or other tangible property. [10] This law only applies if you kept the property because you actually intended to steal it though. [11] Simply forgetting to return a leased automobile is not larceny.

18. How much time can someone get for not returning rented or leased cars or other property?

It depends on the value of the car or property. The larceny punishment schedule is explained in the answer to question #4.

19. So intentionally refusing to give back a $30,000.00 truck could get someone sent to prison for up to 10 years?

Yes. And if the person has a prior history of doing it or if they do it more than once in a single year, they could face even larger sentences.

Chapter 3

Larceny from a Building

20. If a house or building is vacant, is it legal to remove scrap metals or other items from it?

No. Larceny from a vacant dwelling is a misdemeanor that is punishable by imprisonment for up to 1 year or a fine of up to $1,000.00. [12] An important point to remember about this law is that any theft or damage done to a vacant structure or building directly applies to this law. [13]

21. What is the difference between "simple" larceny and larceny from a building?

Simple larceny is theft that has no additional elements attached to it. For example, stealing a radio at the beach might be considered simple theft; however, stealing that radio out of a house is a special category of larceny called larceny from a building, which is a felony. "Any person who shall commit the crime of larceny by stealing in any dwelling house, house trailer, office, store, gasoline service station, shop, warehouse, mill, factory, hotel, school, barn, granary, ship, boat, vessel, church, house of worship, locker room or any building used by the public shall be guilty of a felony." [14] This means stealing in almost any building is automatically a felony.

22. So if I break into a building and steal just $1.00, it is still a felony?

If you break into a building, that alone is a very serious felony. Breaking and entering and home invasion are worse than larceny or larceny from a building because they involve going into someone else's building with the intent of stealing something or committing some other crime. Breaking and entering and home invasion are covered in volume 2 of this collection. The main difference, however, between those crimes and larceny from a building is that, in larceny from a building the thief is allowed to be in the building. For example, at lunch break a worker might steal something from the office. This would be larceny from a building; however, if the worker snuck into the closed office, in the middle of the night, to steal something, it would be breaking and entering.

23. So the person that is guilty of larceny from a building is allowed to be in the building?

Yes.

24. So if I steal $1.00 in a building, is it a felony?

Yes. "Larceny in a building [is] a felony regardless of amounts involved." [15] In People v. Jackson the court distinguished between simple larceny and larceny in a building, and it found that the law makers made larceny from a building a felony because it dealt with "separate social evils" that plain larceny did not deal with. [16]

Think about the problem of shoplifting: people are tempted to steal when they shop, and punishments for low-cost items are up to 93 days in jail if the larceny schedule is applied. However, prosecutors can now apply the larceny within a building law to turn shoplifting into a felony that might carry years of incarceration. [17]

25. Suppose I want to use something that does not belong to me and I take it but I honestly intend to return it later. Is that larceny?

Yes. Your intention to return the property later is not justification for takingstealingit. If the owner does not give you permission to take the item, you are not allowed to take it. The law is as simple as that.

26. What are some real life examples of larceny from a building?

In People v. Williams, the defendant (i.e., Williams) was stealing some merchandise, and she decided not to remove it from the building. In fact, she abandoned the plan and the merchandise. However, she was nevertheless found guilty of larceny from a building because success or failure of an attempt is irrelevant to the question of whether she engaged in larceny while in a building. [18] So we can see here that actually getting out of a building is not necessary to be convicted of larceny from a building.

In another case a defendant was charged with larceny from a building after he took a "woman's purse containing approximately $10.00 from a table in a bar." [19]

In Freeman v. Meijer, Inc., the defendant argued that he was not stealing from the store when he removed price tags from jackets and soiled them and moved them from one location in the store to another. The court disagreed and said the actions showed felonious intent. [20]

In People v. Thornsbury the defendant shoplifted a $39.95 article of merchandice. The court determined that it "is entirely within the discretion of the prosecutor's office" to decide whether to charge the defendant with simple larceny, a 90-day misdemeanor, or with larceny from a building, a 4-year felony. [21]

In People v. Bonds the defendant received larceny from a building for shoplifting a $35 jacket. [22] There are many cases where people stole some insignificant items only to later be charged and convicted of the felony, larceny from a building.

Chapter 4

Larceny from a Person

27. What is larceny from a person?

Larceny from a person is "stealing from the person of another," which is a felony that is "punishable by imprisonment... [for] not more than 10 years." [23]

28. Ten years is a long time. Does it matter how badly the victim is hurt?

Larceny from a person only applies to nonviolent incidents. [24] If the victim is threatened or struck in any manner, larceny from a person is not applicable. [25]

29. Larceny from a person is nonviolently stealing from someone?

Yes. The important part of this law is that "Michigan law requires a defendant to take property from the physical person or immediate presence of a victim to commit larceny from the person." [26] This means the theft has to be directly from the person or from the area right around them. For example, if you picked someone's pocket, you would be committing larceny from a person. Similarly, you would also be committing larceny from a person if you took their wallet after they set it on a table in front of them.

30. Why is larceny from a person a lesser included offense of armed robbery?

Armed robbery has certain elements that must be established to uphold a conviction. Larceny from a person includes some but not all of the elements of armed robbery. Therefore, someone who is charged with armed robbery might not be found guilty of armed robbery, but they might be found guilty of larceny from a person.

31. What are some real life examples of sentences that people have received for larceny from a person?

In People v. Martin the defendant had a previous offense, and he still received less than a year. [27] Previous offenses can quickly increase sentences from months to years. However, if you are trying to figure out how much time you will get for larceny from a person, it depends on the facts of the case, the judge, the prosecutor, the defense attorney, the victim, the political climate, and a host of other factors. You should understand though, that 10 years is a real possibility. In People v. Moore, a normal case, Moore received 6 to 10 years after he pled guilty to larceny from a person. [28]

32. Instead of stealing from a person directly, what would happen if I acted like I was someone else so that I could get things that were supposed to go to them?

You seem to be describing larceny by false personation, which is punishable as normal larceny (see the answer to question #4). [29] For example, if you collect a $1,000.00 prize by acting like you are someone else, who is the actual winner, you will face up to 5 years in prison.

33. What can happen if I steal someone's mail?

Stealing mail is a very serious federal crime. This book only covers Michigan's laws, which most "street" level crime falls under. However, stealing mail is an easy way to get a lot of time in a federal penitentiary. Each piece of mail can be counted as a separate crime, and judges do not go easy on mail thieves.

Chapter 5

Retail Fraud

34. What is retail fraud?

Retail fraud is a kind of larceny that occurs in stores and other businesses when people steal property from the store. Because larceny from a building, simple larceny, and retail fraud have similarities, prosecutors may not consistently apply the charges. You should note, however, that retail fraud has three degrees all of which are distinguished by the value of the items involved.

Retail fraud usually involves certain kinds of actions that relate to any of the following: (1) efforts to misrepresent the price of the property, (2) efforts to steal the property, or (3) efforts to fraudulently refund or exchange the property. [30]

35. What is an easy way to remember the degrees of retail fraud?

First degree involves stealing or cheating the store out of $1,000.00 in cash or property. [31] Second degree involves stealing or cheating the store out of $200.00 or more but less than $1,000.00 in cash or property. [32] Third degree involves stealing or cheating the store out of less than $200.00 in cash or property. [33]

36. What are some examples of retail fraud?

A common one is tampering with price tags. For example, some thieves change price tags in an effort to pay less for merchandise. Another form of retail fraud is stealing merchandise during regular store hours. Refunding or exchanging store goods that have not been purchased is another example of retail fraud. In all three of these examples the thief attempts to either steal the store's property, get it for less than the retail price, or obtain money or something else for it.

37. If someone has already been convicted of retail fraud or a similar crime, can their sentence be enhanced?

Yes. [34]

38. How much time can I get for retail fraud if I do not have any prior convictions for larceny or related crimes?

Third degree retail fraud is a misdemeanor that carries up to 93 days in jail or a fine of not more than $500.00, or both. [35] Second degree retail fraud is also a misdemeanor that carries up to 1 year in jail or a fine of more than $2,000.00, or both. [36] First degree retail fraud is a felony that carries up to 5 years in prison or a fine of not more than $10,000.00, or both. [37]

[Note: The judge can issue a fine, in all three of the degrees of retail fraud, for up to three times the amount that was stolen or attempted to be illegally acquired. For example, someone who attempts to return a $900.00 stolen item for a refund can be fined up to $2,700.00 in addition to up to 1 year in jail.]

39. Is it true that you can be sent to prison for up to 5 years if you commit a second degree [misdemeanor] retail fraud once you have a first degree retail fraud, false pretenses over $100.00, larceny over $100.00, or larceny from a building conviction on your record?

Yes. For repeat offenders a second degree retail fraud can send them to prison for several years. [38]

NOTES

1. MCLS 750.356 (1)(a-g)

2. MCLS 750.356 (2)

3. MCLS 750.356 (3)

4. MCLS 750.356 (4)

5. MCLS 750.356 (5)

6. MCLS 750.356 (7)

7. MCLS 750.356a (1)

8. MCLS 750.356a (2)(b)(ii); MCLS 750.356a (2)(c)(ii); MCLS 750.356a (2)(d)(ii)

9. MCLS 750.356a (3)

10. MCLS 750.362a (1)

11. id.

12. MCLS 750.359

13. id.

14. MCLS 750.360

15. People v. Graves, 31 Mich. App. 635, 1971 Mich. App. LEXIS 2135 (Mich. Ct. App. 1971).

16. People v. Jackson, 29 Mich. App. 654, 1971 Mich. App. LEXIS 2017 (Mich. Ct. App. 1971).

17. People v. Hart, 98 Mich. App. 273, 1980 Mich. App. LEXIS 2744 (Mich. Ct. App. 1980).

18. People v. Williams, 63 Mich. App. 531, 1975 Mich. App. LEXIS 1198 (Mich. Ct. App. 1975).

19. People v. Bohm, 49 Mich. App. 244, 1973 Mich. App. LEXIS 818 (Mich. Ct. App. 1973).

20. Freeman v. Meijer, Inc., 95 Mich. App. 475, 1980 Mich. App. LEXIS 2485 (Mich. Ct. App. 1980).

21. People v. Thornsbury, 148 Mich. App. 92, 1985 Mich. App. LEXIS 3147 (Mich. Ct. App. 1985).

22. People v. Bonds, 121 Mich. App. 233, 1982 Mich. App. LEXIS 3635 (Mich. Ct. App. 1982).

23. MCLS 750.357

24. People v. Tolliver, 46 Mich. App. 34, 1973 Mich. App. LEXIS 1166 (Mich. Ct. App. 1973).

25. id.

26. People v. Anthony, 494 Mich. 669, 2013 Mich. LEXIS 1133 (Mich. 2013).

27. People v. Martin, 257 Mich. App. 457, 2003 Mich. App. LEXIS 1651 (Mich. Ct. App. 2003).

28. People v. Moore, 40 Mich. App. 383, 1972 Mich. App. LEXIS 1225 (Mich. Ct. App. 1972).

29. MCLS 750.363

30. MCLS 750.356c (1)(a-c)

31. id.

32. MCLS 750.356d (1)(a-c)

33. MCLS 750.356d (4)(a-c)

34. MCLS 750.356c (2)

35. MCLS 750.356d (4)

36. MCLS 750.356d (1)

37. MCLS 750.356c (1)

38. People v. Eilola, 179 Mich. App. 315, 1989 Mich. App. LEXIS 386 (Mich. Ct. App. 1989); People v. Brown, 186 Mich. App. 350, 1990 Mich. App. LEXIS 449 (Mich. Ct. App. 1990) ("A prior conviction... may be used not only to raise an act which otherwise would be second-degree retail fraud to first-degree retail fraud, but also to establish the defendant's status as an habitual offender.")

INDEX

Index numbers refer to question numbers, not to page numbers.

12-month period: 8

actual value: 10

armed robbery: 30

barn: 21

boat: 21

breaking and entering: 22

church: 21

damaging vehicle during theft: 16

degrees of retail fraud: 35, 38, 39

dollar value: 3, 5, 6

dwelling: 21

enhanced sentence: 7, 14, 37

factory: 21

felony: 9, 21, 22, 24, 26

home invasion: 22

hotel: 21

house trailer: 21

intent: 22, 26

larceny by false personation: 32

larceny from a building: 3, 21-24, 26, 34

larceny from a motor vehicle: 12, 16, 17

larceny from a person: 3, 27-29, 31

larceny/theft/stealing: 1-13, 15-18, 20-22, 25-30, 32, 34-36, 38

lesser included offenses: 30

locker room: 21

nonviolent: 28

not returning leased/rented vehicles: 17, 18

prior convictions: 7, 14, 19, 31, 38, 39

prison sentences for larceny: 4

prosecutor's discretion: 26

refunding or exchanging store goods: 36

retail fraud: 34, 37, 38

scheme or course of conduct: 8

school: 21

scrap metals: 20

shoplifting: 24, 26

"simple" larceny: 24, 26, 34

stealing mail: 33

store: 21

success or failure is irrelevant: 26

tampering with price tags: 26, 36

threatening or striking: 28

vacant buildings: 20

value of property: 8, 34

7.

Stolen, Embezzled, or Converted Property

Chapter 1 Stolen Property 179

Chapter 2 Chop Shops 189

Notes 193

Index 195

CHAPTER 1

STOLEN PROPERTY

1. If I do not steal something, but I have something that is stolen, can I get in trouble?

Yes. Michigan law prohibits possession of stolen property. In fact, "A person shall not buy, receive, possess, conceal, or aid in the concealment of stolen, embezzled, or converted money, goods, or property knowing, or having reason to know or reason to believe, that the money, goods, or property is stolen, embezzled, or converted." [1]

2. What does that actually mean?

It means all of the following activities are illegal: (1) buying stolen property; (2) accepting stolen property from someone; (3) having or possessing stolen property; (4) hiding or concealing stolen property; (5) helping someone hide or conceal stolen, embezzled, or converted money or property.

All of that just means that it is a crime to use stolen money or property to benefit yourself or someone else. Because there are so many ways that a person might attempt to use stolen money or property, this law is very broad. The point of the law is to deter people from possessing or helping someone possess or use stolen money or property.

3. What is the punishment for receiving and concealing stolen property?

The punishments depend on the dollar value of the stolen property and whether the offender has prior convictions for certain related crimes. You can get up to 10 years or a fine of up to three times the value of the property or up to $15,000.00, or both--the prison sentence and fine--for property valued at $20,000.00 or more. [2] However, you can get the same sentence for property valued at $1,000.00 or more but less than $20,000.00 if you have two or more prior convictions for related crimes. [3]

4. So I can get up to 10 years each for my first and second offenses of $20,000.00, but for the third offense I can get up to 10 years for something that is only worth $1,000.00?

Yes. The third offense, for expensive items, is the one where the value of the property can be much less, but you will still be facing a large prison sentence or fine, or both.

5. Suppose I have less than $20,000.00 items. What sort of prison sentences would I face?

You can get up to 5 years or a fine of up to three times the value of the property or up to $10,000.00, or both (i.e., the prison sentence and fine) for property valued at $1,000.00 or more but less than $20,000.00. [4] However, you can get the same sentence for property valued at $200.00 or more but less than $1,000.00 if you have 1 or more prior convictions for related crimes. [5]

6. So if I steal something that costs $1,762.39, I can get up to 5 years in prison?

Yes.

7. And I will face the same sentence on my very next offense even though the value of the property will go down to about $200.00--$1,000.00?

Yes. After the first conviction, you will be subject to as much time in prison as people who have clean records. However, you will be in jeopardy of getting a 5-year sentence for being in possession of property that is only valued at $200.00--$1,000.00 while people with clean records won't get that much time unless they have stolen property that is valued at approximately $1,000.00--$20,000.00.

8. How much time could I get for stealing property valued at less than $1,000.00?

Larceny law covers theft. Being in possession of stolen property and actually stealing are two completely different offenses. We will cover this again later.

9. If I am in possession of stolen items that are valued at $200.00 or more but less than $1,000.00, how much time can I get?

Up to a year in jail, a $2,000.00 fine or three times the value of the property, or both. [6] However, if this is your second offense, you can get a year in jail for being in possession of stolen property that is valued at less than $200.00. [7]

10. Suppose I am just a petty thief stealing items that cost less than $200.00; what kind of sentence would I face?

Again, larceny, which is theft, is a different crime than possessing stolen property, which is the subject covered in this book.

11. okay, we are not discussing theft; what sort of sentence can I get for having stolen property that is worth less than $200.00?

You can get up to 93 days in jail, a fine of $500.00 or three times the value of the stolen property, or both. [8] The law here does not state what might happen to a person if they have prior convictions. Readers here should assume that other laws will be applied to make the punishment more severe for repeat offenders.

12. If someone bought stolen property regularly, how would that be dealt with if they got caught?

The total value of the stolen would be calculated for the past year to determine how much imprisonment the person would face if convicted. [9]

13. If I buy a stolen car for $900.00, I can get up to 1 year in prison?

No. Vehicles are a special category of stolen property that is protected more than most property. If you buy or possess or help someone else buy or possess a stolen vehicle, regardless of the vehicle's value, you will automatically be in danger of being sentenced to up to 5 years in prison or a fine of 3 times the value of the vehicle or up to $10,000.00, or both. A second offense carries up to 10 years in prison or a fine of up to $15,000.00 or 3 times the value of the vehicle, or both. [10]

14. If someone were to change the serial numbers or scratch them out on an item, how could anyone ever prove the item is stolen?

In law, the assumption is that people alter or obliterate serial numbers to avoid prosecution. [11] So, if you change or deface the serial numbers on something, the authorities will assume the property is stolen, and you will have to try to convince a judge or jury that the property is not stolen.

15. Can people at pawn shops buy property that has the serial numbers removed?

Dealers who purchase "property with external serial numbers or other identifying numbers altered or obliterated shall be presumed to have bought such property with knowledge that it was stolen." [12] This means the burden is then on the person to explain why he or she should not be found guilty of receiving and concealing stolen property. This scenario extends to common people too: if you purchase something that has the serial number altered or obliterated, people can assume that you know or believe the property is stolen. You do not have to know the details of where the property was stolen from or such to suspect the property is stolen, and that is what the law expects from you. [13]

16. If someone brings me a $500.00 piece of equipment and offers it to me for $20.00, I'm going to buy it. Are you saying that I can be charged for that?

No. I am saying that you should be careful when purchasing items that have suspicious circumstances attached to them. "The circumstances accompanying a transaction may justify [the belief] by the jury that the defendant received the goods on belief that they were stolen." [14]

17. How can I know whether something is stolen or not?

You have to ask yourself whether you would offer someone such a great deal if you were the seller and the property was legally yours. You also have to ask questions and try to determine whether the property was stolen. Basically, you have to legitimately try to avoid purchasing or acquiring stolen property. If you don't do these things or similar ones, a jury could look at the circumstances of your case and infer that you received the goods with the belief that they were stolen. [15]

18. What is guilt knowledge?

Guilt knowledge is knowledge that you pick up by paying attention to the details of a situation to determine whether something illegal is occurring. [16] Guilt knowledge is actually an "essential element required to be proved in order to establish the offense of receiving and concealing stolen property." [17]

19. How can anyone know you have guilt knowledge?

No one can ever be absolutely sure of another person's knowledge unless that person honestly tells what they know; however, the law allows jurors to imagine themselves in the defendant's position when the crime was committed. If the jurors come away from that experience believing they would have known the property was stolen or that you should have known it was stolen, "guilt knowledge may fairly be [established]. [18]

20. Are there other ways to know whether a defendant has guilt knowledge/

Yes. The "essential element of guilt knowledge generally must be inferred from all circumstances of [the] case" including whether the defendant attempted to change the condition of the property, tampered with the serial numbers, obtained the property far below market value, and could not provide good explanation for possessing the property. [19] This means jurors will consider the circumstances that led up to the possession of the property, as well as the circumstances that followed it, to determine whether they believe the defendant probably knew the property was stolen.

21. Suppose I buy a cheap little stolen pistol for $50.00, and I get caught with it; I will only get 93 days in jail if I don't have any prior convictions, right?

Wrong. Firearms are another exception to the stolen property laws. The law actually says you will be facing up to 10 years for a stolen firearm or stolen ammunition that you "receive, conceal, store, barter, sell, dispose of, pledge, or accept as security for a loan." [20] In addition to this, the firearm laws also apply which automatically give you a 2-year nonparolable prison sentence for felony firearm (i.e., possession of a firearm while committing another felony, which in this case is the receiving of the stolen firearm) which has to be served separate from the sentence for receiving a stolen firearm. This is a particularly dangerous crime because under certain circumstances you could receive up to 10 years in prison for each stolen gun that you buy, sell, receive, or otherwise become involved with.

22. Can you get 10 years for buying, selling, or both?

Both. The law is strict about firearms, especially stolen firearms. Any felony committed with a firearm automatically get the defendant sent to prison for a minimum of 2 years, just for having a firearm present during the commission of a felony.

23. Can a person be convicted on circumstantial evidence of receiving and concealing stolen property?

Yes. [21]

Chapter 2

Chop Shops

24. What is a chop shop?

Any building or location where 1 or more people are "altering, dismantling, reassembling, or in any way concealing or disguising the identity of a stolen motor vehicle or of any major component part of a stolen motor vehicle" is a chop shop. [22] A chop shop is also defined in law as "any [area] where there are 3 or more stolen motor vehicles [] or where there are major component parts from 3 or more stolen motor vehicles present." [23]

25. What is meant by major component part?

The engine, the transmission, the doors, the fenders, the hood, the bumpers, the quarter panels, the cab, the tailgate, an airbag, a wheel or tire, and related parts. [24] Some people might have stolen property on their property, and those parts could be used to prosecute the person for operating a chop shop.

26. How much time can a person get for operating a chop shop?

Operating and assisting someone in the operation of a chop shop is "punishable by imprisonment for not more than 10 years or a fine of not more than $250,000.00, or both. [25] The second offense for operating or assisting in the operation of a chop shop carries the same prison time, but it also includes a minimum $10,000.00 fine if the judge decides to issue a fine, or both. [26]

27. If someone gets convicted of receiving and concealing stolen property, do they have to pay restitution?

Restitution, which is paying the victim back for their loss, is something a judge can order in addition to a sentence and/or a fine, but the law does not specifically require judges to do so. However, judges are required to order restitution when people are convicted of operating a chop shop. [27] This means you will have to pay back the original owners or the insurance company for every stolen vehicle or auto part that you get caught with.

28. Drug dealers often lose their homes, money, cars, and other property when they get convicted. Are there laws in place to seize people's property if they get caught operating a chop shop?

Yes. A long list of property can be seized, but a short list includes parts and vehicles used in the operation, all records, money, properties, and tools. [28] This basically means the person accused of operating a chop shop can lose most of their money and property.

29. What happens to confiscated property?

A hearing is held to determine whether it is stolen or your lawful possession. if it is yours, you get it back. If it is not, it gets sold at auction or otherwise disposed of. [29]

Notes

1. MCLS 750.535

2. MCLS 750.535 (2)(a)

3. MCLS 750.535 (2)(b)

4. MCLS 750.535 (3)(a)

5. MCLS 750.535 (3)(b)

6. MCLS 750.535 (4)(a)

7. MCLS 750.535 (4)(b)

8. MCLS 750.535 (5)

9. MCLS 750.535 (6)

10. MCLS 750.535 (7-8)

11. People v. Gallagher, 404 Mich. 429, 1979 Mich. LEXIS 419 (Mich. 1979).

12. id.

13. People v. Brown, 126 Mich. App. 282, 1983 Mich. App. LEXIS 3041 (Mich. Ct. App. 1983).

14. id.

15. People v. Wolak, 110 Mich. App. 628, 1981 Mich. App. LEXIS 3364 (Mich. Ct. App. 1981); People v. Goble, 2009 Mich. App. LEXIS 1293 (Mich. Ct. App. June 11, 2009).

16. People v. Tantenella, 212 Mich. 614, 1920 Mich. LEXIS 557 (Mich. 1920); Echelon Homes, L.L.C. v. Carter Lumber Co., 472 Mich. 192, 2005 Mich. LEXIS 443 (Mich. 2005).

17. People v. Westerfield, 71 Mich. App. 618, 1976 Mich. App. LEXIS 991 (Mich. Ct. App. 1976).

18. People v. White, 22 Mich. App. 65, 1970 Mich. App. LEXIS 1943 (Mich. Ct. App. 1970).

19. People v. Salata, 79 Mich. App. 415, 1977 Mich. App. LEXIS 784 (Mich. Ct. App. 1977).

20. MCLS 750.535b (1-2)

21. People v. Blackwell, 61 Mich. App. 236, 1975 Mich. App. LEXIS 1523 (Mich. Ct. App. 1975) ("A conviction may rest on evidence which is purely circumstantial in nature.")

22. MCLS 750.535a (1)(b)(i)

23. MCLS 750.535a (1)(b)(ii)

24. MCLS 750.535a (1)(c)(i-xvi)

25. MCLS 750.535a (2)

26. MCLS 750.535a (3)

27. MCLS 750.535a (4)

28. MCLS 750.535a (5)(a-d)

29. MCLS 750.535a (6-15)

INDEX

Index numbers refer to question numbers, not to page numbers.

auction: 29

chop shop:

--assisting: 26

--definition: 24

circumstances accompanying a transaction: 16, 20, 21

circumstantial evidence: 23

confiscated property: 29

drug dealers: 28

felony firearm: 21

firearms: 21, 22

guilt knowledge: 18-20

inference: 16, 17, 19, 20

insurance company: 27

larceny: 8, 10, 11

major component part: 24, 25

pawn shop: 15

prior conviction(s):

--first offense: 4, 7

--second offense: 4, 9, 13, 26
--third offense: 4
restitution: 27
serial number: 14, 15, 20
stolen property/money:
--aiding or assisting in crime: 1, 2
--ammunition: 21
--buying: 1, 2, 17
--changing condition of: 20
--concealing: 1-3, 15, 18, 21, 23, 27
--converting: 1, 2
--disposing of: 21
--dollar value: 3, 8, 12
--embezzling: 1, 2
--firearm: 21, 22
--obtained below market value: 20
--possessing: 1, 2, 8-11
--receiving: 1-3, 15, 17, 18, 21, 27
--selling: 21
--vehicle(s): 13, 27
suspicious circumstances: 16, 20, 21

8.

Malicious and Wilful Mischief and Destruction

Chapter 1 Malicious Destruction of Property..199

Chapter 2 Destruction to Signs, Lights, Fences, and Memorials 203

Chapter 3 Destruction to Property: Police Dept., Fire Dept., Trains, School Buses 205

Chapter 4 Destruction To Utilities, Logs and Timber, and Mining Machinery 207

Chapter 5 Destruction to Ships, Bridges, and Dams 211

Chapter 6 Destruction to Houses, Barns, Crops, and Trees 213

Notes 215

Index 217

CHAPTER 1

MALICIOUS DESTRUCTION OF PROPERTY

1. What is malicious destruction of property?

Malicious destruction of property is a crime. It occurs when a person intentionally injures or destroys another person's property. [1]

2. What is the punishment for malicious destruction of property?

The punishment depends on 2 factors: (1) the dollar value of the injury or destruction to the property and (2) whether you have prior malicious destruction convictions. The following punishment schedule applies to most instances of malicious destruction of property; however, several exceptions will be discussed later.

"A felony punishable by imprisonment for not more than 10 years or a fine of not more than $15,000.00 or 3 times the amount of the [damage], whichever is greater, or both imprisonment and a fine" applies to the damages of $20,000.00 or more. [2] This 10 year maximum sentence and fine also applies to anyone with 2 or more prior malicious destruction convictions who gets convicted of another one, even if the priors and the new conviction are for much less than $20,000.00. [3]

"A felony punishable by imprisonment for not more than 5 years or a fine of not more than $10,000.00 or 3 times the amount of the [damage], whichever is greater, or both imprisonment and a fine" applies to damages of $1,000.00 or more but not less than $20,000.00. [4] This 5 year maximum sentence and fine also applies to anyone with 1 or more malicious destruction convictions who gets convicted of another one, even if the priors and the new conviction are for much less than $1,000.00. [5]

Up to a 1-year misdemeanor and/or fine applies to damages of $200.00 or more but less than $1,000.00. [6] This sentence also applies to anyone with a prior malicious destruction conviction who gets convicted of another one, even if the new conviction is [only a local city or town rule] that relates to the Michigan malicious destruction laws. [7]

Up to a 93-day misdemeanor and/or fine applies to damages of less than $200.00. [8]

3. If someone repeatedly damages someone else's property, will all of the damages be calculated together to determine how much time they will face?

Yes, it can be done that way if the prosecutor chooses to take that approach. So, for example, a person who broke $400.00 in windows in January, $500.00 in machinery in March, and $300.00 in yard furniture in August can face up to 5 years in prison even though the individual crimes are 1-year misdemeanors. [8]

Chapter 2

Destruction to Signs, Lights, Fences, and Memorials

4. A friend of mine said it is a misdemeanor to spray paint stop signs. Is that true?

Yes. The first offense could result in up to 93 days in jail; the second offense, up to 180 days in jail; and the third or more offenses, up to 1 year in jail. [9] A stop sign is a traffic control device. The law prohibits damaging, destroying, injuring, defacing, dismantling, tampering with, or removing traffic control devices.

5. What are other traffic control devices?

"A sign, signal, electronic traffic control sign or signal, marking, light post, railroad sign or signal, or [similar] device." [10] You might also benefit from knowing that the law also anticipates people getting hurt, possibly killed, if you tamper with traffic control devices. The law specifically says that, in addition to being charged for, convicted of, and sentenced for destruction to traffic control devices, you can also be "charged with, convicted of, or sentenced for any other violation of law arising" from the damage to the traffic control device. [11]

6. So I can be held responsible if someone runs over a little kid because the traffic control device that I tampered with did not work right?

Yes.

7. Just for fun I have kicked or broken fences and gates. Is that a crime?

To "break down, injure, mar or deface any fence belonging to [someone else]" is a misdemeanor. [12]

8. I have heard of kids going to cemeteries to knock down gravestones and vandalize the grounds. How much trouble can they get in if they get caught?

See the answer to question #2 above. The punishment depends on the amount of damage done and whether prior convictions will increase the punishments

Chapter 3

Destruction to Property: Police Dept., Fire Dept., Trains, School Buses

9. Is it true that all destruction of police and fire department property is a felony?

Yes. [13] There are no "minor" offenses when it comes to damaging police and fire department property. Because police and fire department property is often used to save lives, damage to that property is very serious, regardless of the amount of damage involved.

10. Is it true that damaging, destroying, or altering school buses is a felony too?

Yes. In fact, you can get up to 5 years in prison for it. [14]

11. If I only let the air out of the tires, without actually damaging them, would that count?

Yes. Deflating the tires is altering the school bus, and altering the bus is prohibited.

12. What is the law about throwing rocks and other dangerous objects at automobiles?

The following applies to trains and automobiles. Throwing dangerous objects (e.g., rocks) is a misdemeanor punishable by imprisonment for up to 93 days and/or up to a $1,000.00 fine. [15] This is only for the act of throwing something at a train or automobile. If you actually hit and damage one of them, the punishment increases to up to 1 year and/or up to a $500.00 fine. [16]

If someone gets injured as a result of you throwing something at a train or automobile, you will face a felony punishable by imprisonment for up to 4 years and/or up to a $2,000.00 fine. [17] If the person gets seriously injured, you will face up to 10 years and/or up to a $5,000.00 fine. [18] And if someone dies, you will face up to 15 years and/or up to a $10,000.00 fine. [19]

You might be wondering how a rock could cause someone in a car to die. Among other ways, a person might turn into oncoming traffic if the rock suddenly hits their windshield. We can never know for sure how another person is going to react when they are surprised while operating a motor vehicle.

Chapter 4

Destruction To Utilities, Logs and Timber, and Mining Machinery

13. What is a utility?

In the of law pertaining to malicious destruction, utility "includes any pipeline, gas, electric, heat, water, oil, sewer, telephone, telegraph, telecommunication, radio, railway, railroad, airplane, transportation, communication or other system, whether or not publicly owned, that is operated for the public use." [20]

14. If someone cuts or breaks or tampers with or defaces a utility, is that a misdemeanor?

No. It is a felony that is punishable by up to 5 years in prison or up to a $5,000.00 fine, or both. [21] Utilities include all of the machinery, tools, equipment, line, post, towers, pipe, valves, appliances, components, and property of the people, community, and/or organization that provides the product of the utility for public use. [22]

15. Does this apply to tempering with power lines?

Yes. Virtually any device or equipment that provides electricity, water, sewage removal, heat, communications service, and other utilities is protected. [23]

16. Someone told me it is illegal to drive nails into trees. Is that true?

It is a misdemeanor to maliciously injure logs or timber. [24] That means intentionally driving or embedding metal objects into logs or trees that are likely to be sent to a mill yard to be made into lumber is a crime. This is a crime because, among other things, the metal objects damage the mill blades.

17. Some protesters are planning to sneak into a mine and destroy some of the equipment to interrupt the mining. Is that a misdemeanor or a felony?

That is a very serious felony that carries up to a 20 year prison sentence. [25]

18. Why does destruction of mining equipment have such a severe punishment?

Mining is dangerous work, and the equipment is used to save lives when needed. Tampering with the equipment can cause someone to be placed in mortal danger or unable to be rescued from such danger.

Chapter 5

Destruction to Ships, Bridges, and Dams

19. Are boats, ships, and other water bound vessels treated the same as automobiles when they are maliciously damaged?

No. For some reason lawmakers have given boats, ships, and other such vessels and the property on such vessels a more severe punishment than for most destruction offenses to automobiles. [26]

20. How is the punishment more severe?

Any malicious destruction to a vessel is automatically a felony that is punishable by imprisonment for up to 10 years. [27]

21. Is there an option to get a fine instead?

No. The guilty person is going to prison.

22. So destroying or sinking a boat is punishable by up to 10 years in prison?

Yes. But the law does not stop there: if you injure any of the property onboard a vessel, you will also face up to 10 years in prison. [28]

23. Is damage to a bridge a misdemeanor or a felony?

A felony. The bridge and everything connected to the bridge, railroad, dam, and canal are all protected. Damaging them places people's lives in jeopardy, and the law punishes such activity severely.

24. What about dams and canals is against the law?

The destruction, damage, or tampering with the components of a dam, canal, reservoir, trench, levee or structure intended for the conveying of water to or from a dam or reservoir is a felony. [30] This includes the wheels, gears, and machinery of any mill that uses water from such dams or reservoirs. [31]

Chapter 6

Destruction to Houses, Barns, Crops, and Trees

25. What kind of punishment does the law have for damaging or destroying someone's house?

Intentionally damaging or destroying someone else's house, barn, or other building falls under the punishment schedule described in the answer to question #2 above. [32]

26. So I could get up to 10 years for $20,000.00 or more in damages to someone's house, garage, barn, or shed?

Yes.

27. Suppose I offered to clean up the damage. What would happen then?

When someone calls the police, the state of Michigan gets involved. That means the matter is no longer between just you and the other person. When the state gets involved, it wants to know who broke its laws. Whether you repair the damage or not does not excuse the fact that you broke the law.

28. So if I am going to get caught, I might as well damage as much as possible because I am going to go to jail anyway. Is that what you are saying?

No. The more you damage, the more the potential sentence will be. Judges see malicious destruction cases often. However, people who lose control and become especially destructive motive the judge to give them large sentences. On the other hand, people who accept responsibility, attempt to make amends, and demonstrate that they are under control provide the judge with reasons to sentence them to the lower end of the sentencing guidelines or even just a fine.

29. Is it true that you can go to jail for injuring or destroying people's crops and trees?

Yes. The punishment schedule is in the answer to #2 above, but you can definitely go to jail or prison if the damage is extensive enough. The law specifically prohibits cutting down, destroying or injuring "any tree, shrub, grass, turf, plants, crops, or soil of another." [33]

NOTES

1. MCLS 750.377a (1)
2. MCLS 750.377a (1)(a)(i)
3. MCLS 750.377a (1)(a)(ii)
4. MCLS 750.377a (1)(b)(i)
5. MCLS 750.377a (1)(b)(ii)
6. MCLS 750.377a (1)(c)(i)
7. MCLS 750.377a (1)(c)(ii)
8. MCLS 750.377a (2)
9. MCLS 750.377d (1)(a-c)
10. MCLS 750.377d (3)
11. MCLS 750.377d (2)
12. MCLS 750.381
13. MCLS 750.377b
14. MCLS 750.377c
15. MCLS 750.394 (1-2)
16. id.
17. id.
18. id.

19. id.

20. MCLS 750.383a

21. id.

22. id.

23. id.

24. MCLS 750.384

25. MCLS 750.386

26. MCLS 750.392

27. id.

28. id.

29. MCLS 750.379

30. id.

31. id.

32. MCLS 750.380

33. MCLS 750.382

INDEX

Index numbers refer to question numbers, not to page numbers.

death: 12

dollar value of the property: 2

double punishment: 22

felony: 2, 9, 10, 12, 14, 17, 20, 23, 24

malicious destruction of property:

--automobiles: 12

--cemetaries: 8

--house, barn, crops, and trees: 25, 26

--"just for fun": 7

--logs and timber: 16

--mining machinery: 17, 18

--police and fire department

--powerlines: 15

--school buses: 9-11

--ships, bridges, dams: 19, 23

--signs, lights, fences, and memorials: 4, 7, 8

--stop signs: 4

--traffic control device: 4-6

--trains: 9, 12

--utilities: 13-15

mandatory prison term: 21

offers to pay for the damages: 27, 28

prior convictions: 2, 8

prosecutor's discretion: 3

punishment schedule: 2, 25, 28, 29

repeatedly damaging property: 3

serious injuries: 12

tampering: 4-6, 14, 15, 18, 24

throwing rocks: 12

9.

Miscellaneous Offenses

Chapter 1 Kidnapping, Stalking, Illegal Computer Posting, Disorderly Conduct 221

Chapter 2 Ethnic Intimidation, Terrorism, Filing False Reports 231

Chapter 3 Criminal Enterprises, Gangs, Hazing, Conspiracy, Attempts 237

Chapter 4 Uttering and Publishing, Forgery, and Counterfeiting 247

Chapter 5 Arson 251

Notes 259

Index 265

Chapter 1

Kidnapping, Stalking, Illegal Computer Posting, Disorderly Conduct

1. What is kidnapping?

Kidnapping is an extremely serious felony that occurs when someone restrains someone else for the purpose of doing any of the following: (1) holding the person for ransom, (2) using the person as a hostage, (3) raping or molesting the person, (4) taking the person out of Michigan, (5) forcing the person to work, or (6) sexually abusing the person [#6 specifically applies to children]. [1]

2. What is the punishment for kidnapping?

Imprisonment for life or any term of years or a fine of not more than $50,000.00, or both. [2]

3. What is unlawful imprisonment?

Unlawful imprisonment is a felony similar to kidnapping; however, it does not require as much to be convicted of it. The crime occurs if one uses a weapon or dangerous instrument to restrain another person, to keep someone secretly confined, or to make someone help them commit a crime or flee a crime. [3] This means pulling a weapon out on someone and telling them to stay where they are or to go somewhere against their will is unlawful imprisonment. So is locking someone in a room or other location against their will. Forcing someone to participate in any part of a crime is also unlawful imprisonment. [4]

4. Is it still unlawful imprisonment if you just force someone at gunpoint to drive you somewhere?

That is a very serious offense. Yes. Forcing someone at gunpoint to drive you somewhere is unlawful imprisonment. [5]

5. Suppose I don't have a weapon and I just use my size to control them. Could that be unlawful imprisonment?

Based on how the law reads, I would be inclined to say no, but there are Michigan cases that fit that description. For instance, in one case the defendant was convicted of unlawful imprisonment for blocking the doorway when the victim attempted to leave and for grabbing her arm, taking her keys, and throwing them out into the yard. [6]

6. What is the punishment for unlawful imprisonment?

Not more than 15 years imprisonment and/or up to a $20,000.00 fine. [7]

7. How does the law define stalking?

Stalking is defined as "conduct involving repeated or continuing harassment of another individual that would cause a reasonable person to feel terrorized, frightened, intimidated, threatened, harassed, or molested" and the victim confirms feeling that way due to the perpetrator's actions. [8]

8. Does that mean someone can say they feel threatened or intimidated by me, and because that is the way they feel, I can be convicted of stalking?

No. A stalking conviction hinges on 2 important elements: (1) the victim must feel emotional distress (e.g., to feel frightened) as a result of the action in question and (2) that emotional distress must be what a reasonable person would feel under such circumstances. Therefore, if either is missing, stalking has not occurred. For example, if the victim does not feel emotional distress, even though a reasonable person would, stalking has not occurred. Likewise, if a victim feels emotional distress, though a reasonable person would not, stalking has not occurred.

9. What is the punishment for stalking?

If the victim is an adult, the misdemeanor punishment is up to 1 year in jail and/or a fine of up to $1,000.00. However, if the victim is a juvenile and the defendant is 5 or more years older than the victim, the punishment is imprisonment for up to 5 years and/or a fine of up to $10,000.00. [9]

10. Are there any alternatives to getting fined or incarcerated following a stalking conviction?

The judge is given an option to place the offender on up to 5 years of probation that could include going to counseling or therapy at the offender's expense. [10]

11. To be clear, what are some actions that could be seen as stalking?

Two or more separate episodes of any of the following could be grounds for stalking charges, especially if the victim expresses a desire for the behavior to cease: (1) following the victim, (2) approaching or confronting the victim in public or private, (3) appearing at the victim's workplace or residence, (4) entering onto the victim's property, (5) contacting the victim by telephone or electronic media, and (6) placing an object on the victim's property or delivering an object to the victim. (11)

12. Some of the actions listed above could be random and innocent. How does the law distinguish between stalking and innocent mistakes?

People are expected to be conscious of how they are treating other people and how those people are feeling. If someone expresses a desire to be left alone, you have a responsibility to stop harassing them. If you continue, the police can be called, charges filed, and a trial held to determine whether a reasonable person would feel "terrorized, frightened, intimidated, threatened, harassed, or molested" under such circumstances. If a judge or jury determines you are guilty, the law between stalking and innocent mistakes will have to be distinguished.

13. What is aggravated stalking?

Aggravated stalking occurs when a person participates in regular stalking and during that activity (1) violates a restraining order or injunction or preliminary injunction or (2) violates a probation condition, a parole condition, a pretrial release condition, or an appeal-bond condition or (3) makes a "credible threat [] against the victim, a member of the victim's family, or another individual living in the same household as the victim," or (4) has a prior stalking conviction. [12]

14. How much time can someone get for aggravated stalking?

Up to 5 years and/or up to a $10,000.00 fine. However, if the victim is a juvenile and the perpetrator is 5 or more years older than the victim, the punishment is up to 10 years in prison and/or a $15,000.00 fine. [13] A minimum 5 year probation option is available if the judge wants to use it. [14]

15. Can posting things on social media be used against someone in a stalking case?

Yes. A person might become angry at someone else and post things that make unconsented contact with the intended victim. If those posts make the victim feel "terrorized, frightened, intimidated, threatened, harassed, or molested" and a reasonable person would feel that way due to the content of the posts, the person who posted the material could be in danger of being charged with a felony that is related to stalking but specifically focused on posting messages that are intended to harass and/or terrorize. The crime is punishable by up to 2 years in prison and/or a $5,000.00 fine. If the crime is aggravated (e.g., involving credible threats), the punishment increases to up to 5 years and/or a $10,000.00 fine. [15]

16. Does this mean I can get charged with a felony for using my First Amendment right to free speech?

Threatening people is not protected speech. This law specifically states "This section does not prohibit constitutionally protected speech or activity." [16] However, the First Amendment is not a license to abuse others, and arguing the point in court can be expensive, time consuming, and challenging.

17. What is the disorderly person law?

It is a misdemeanor punishable by not more than 90 days in jail and/or up to a $500.00 fine for being a person who refuses to support his or her family, being a prostitute, being a window peeper, being a person who is intoxicated and causing a public disturbance, being "a person who is engaged in indecent or obscene conduct in a public place," being a vagrant, being a beggar in a public place, being a loiterer in a place where prostitution commonly occurs, being a loiterer in a police station, jail, hospital, court building, or other public building for the purpose of getting people to hire you for legal assistance, and being a person who is pushing people in a crowded public place. [17] The law reads "A person is disorderly if the person...engages in an illegal occupation or business." [18] The first felony for disorderly person can send a person to prison for up to 2 years and/or cost them a fine of up to $5,000.00. Additional felonies for disorderly person offenses carry up to 4 years in prison and/or a $10,000.00 fine. [19]

18. What is gross indecency?

"What constitutes gross indecency involves a question of community morals determinable by a trier of facts." [20] Gross indecency itself is a felony; however, the exact act or acts that constitute gross indecency are not explicitly stated. Therefore, in one area of Michigan a given activity will be tolerated while the same activity in another area of Michigan will be punished as a felony. [21] The law seems to be focusing on sexual activities that would offend the people who might act as a judge or jury over the case. Therefore, to avoid this crime readers would be wise to keep their sexual activities, if any, out of the public eye and within the values of their community. Another way to violate the gross indecency law is to negotiate or organize the commission of any act of gross indecency between 2 or more people.

19. How much time does a conviction for gross indecency carry?

Not more than 5 years and/or a fine of $2,500.00. However, if a person is sexually delinquent at the time of the act of gross indecency the law states that the punishment may be imprisonment "for an indeterminate term, the minimum of which shall be 1 day and the maximum of which shall be life." [22]

Chapter 2

Ethnic Intimidation, Terrorism, Filing False Reports

20. what is ethnic intimidation?

Ethnic intimidation is threat or act to cause "physical contact with another person" or damage to another person's property for the purpose of intimidating or harassing them "because of that person's race, color, religion, gender, or national origin." [23]

21. What is the punishment for ethnic intimidation?

Ethnic intimidation is a felony that can send you to prison for up to 2 years or cost you up to $5,000.00 in a fine, or both. [24] You should also be aware that the ethnic intimidation law says victims may sue offenders for attorney fees and up to 3 times the value of damages regardless of whether the offender is found guilty in the criminal prosecution. [25]

22. What is an example of ethnic intimidation?

Calling someone a racist name and threatening them could be ethnic intimidation because it singles the person's race out and attempts to intimidate or harass them by threat. Another could be writing an offensive comment, about someone's gender, on their house or car. Another could be making reference to someone's religion while fighting with them.

23. What is terrorism?

Terrorism is a crime in which a criminal attempts to intimidate or force the government or a part of the government to function in the way the criminal wants it to function rather than according to the principles of democracy and the accepted policies that are in place according to the will of the people. An act of terrorism then is a violent felony that is likely to be a threat to human life and intended to control or influence a governmental body through fear. [26]

24. How much time in prison can someone get for terrorism?

"Imprisonment for life or any term of years or a fine of not more than $100,000.00, or both." [27] Also, if someone dies as a result of the terrorist act, the criminal "shall be punished by imprisonment for life without the eligibility for parole." [28]

25. I don't understand; what are some examples of terrorism?

Think of any public organization that is funded by taxpayers' dollars, for example, a school, police or fire department, city council, county courthouse, prison, or Secretary of State office. These organizations have a way of operating, but some people do not agree with that methodology. Rather than going through the right channels to change the operating procedures of these organizations, criminals commit violent felonies against the organization such as burning or blowing up their buildings and property to scare them into changing their operations.

26. If I do not commit an act of terrorism but I assist someone else, how bad is that?

Raising support for terrorists or supporting terrorists in any manner is a felony punishable by imprisonment for [up to] 20 years or a fine of [up to] $20,000.00, or both." [29]

27. What does that really mean?

It means that any attempt to collect money or resources or participants for a person or group that plans to commit a terrorist act is a crime that can send you to prison for a very long time. It also means that helping a terrorist or terrorist group to plan, organize, prepare, or otherwise carry out a terrorist act is also a very serious crime that can ruin your life. The smallest amount of assistance, for example, providing a fleeing criminal money, a ride, or instructions, can get you sent to prison for decades. This is an externally dangerous topic that the courts and law enforcement agencies take very seriously. If you engage in any activity of this sort, you could destroy your future and jeopardize your friends and family as well.

28. Suppose someone merely makes a terrorist threat, how dangerous is that?

The law punishes people who make terrorist threats as severely as people who assist terrorists. [30] If you make the threat, the law takes you at your word. Look at the wording here that is taken directly from the law: "It is not a defense to a prosecution under this section that the defendant did not have the intent or capability of committing the act of terrorism." [31]

That means that you will be prosecuted (i.e., arrested, brought to trial, and sentenced if found guilty) if you make a terrorist threat. It does not matter whether you actually have bombs to blow things up or guns to shoot people or whatever else you might need to carry out your threats. All that matters is that you threatened to commit a terrorist act.

29. So I could get 20 years in prison just for threatening to commit a crime?

No. Threatening to commit a random crime is not the same as threatening to commit a terrorist act.

30. Can I get all that time if I call 9-1-1 and falsely report a crime?

Making a false report to a police officer, 9-1-1 operator, or other governmental employee that receives crime reports is a crime, but it is a misdemeanor if the crime being falsely reported is a misdemeanor, and it is a felony if the crime being falsely reported is a felony. The punishments for making a false report is up to 93 days for the misdemeanor and up to 4 years for the felony variety. The punishment increases if someone gets hurt as a result of responding to the false report: up to 5 years if they get hurt, 10 years if they get seriously hurt, and 15 years if they die. [32] In addition, to these sentences, fines and other charges may also apply.

Chapter 3

Criminal Enterprises, Gangs, Hazing, Conspiracy, Attempts

31. What is racketeering?

Racketeering is any conspiracy, attempt, or act- whether made personally or through someone else- to commit a crime for financial gain that involves certain aspects of the law regarding cigerette taxes, disposal of hazardous waste, controlled substances, ephedrine or pseudoephedrine, welfare fraud, medicaid fraud, gaming, alcohol, fraud, pornography, animal fighting, banking instruments, breaking and entering or home invasion, bribery, jury tampering, child sexual abuse or material, internet or computer crimes, credit cards or financial transaction devices, embezzlement, explosives, extortion, false pretenses, firearms or dangerous weapons, forgery and counterfeiting, securities fraud, food stamps or coupons or access devices, gambling, murder, horse racing, kidnapping, larceny, money laundering, perjury, prostitution, human trafficking, robbery, stolen or embezzled or converted property, terrorism, obscenity, identity theft, federal racketeering, or similar topics to the above listed ones. [33]

32. What is a shorter definition of racketeering?

Directly or indirectly breaking certain laws for financial gain.

33. What do you mean by indirectly?

Aiding and abetting, soliciting, coercing, intimidating, or in any other way persuading a person to commit one of the crimes so you can financially gain from it.

34. Suppose I go to work for someone who orders me to do things that are illegal. Can I get in trouble for doing my job?

Yes. The law says a person may "not knowingly conduct or participate in the" racketeering activities of any person or organization. [34] As a Michigan citizen, you are obligated to follow Michigan laws. If you follow criminal instructions from anyone, you can be prosecuted for doing so. No one has the right to order you to break the law, and you will be held responsible if you are caught breaking the law.

35. If I save up money and invest in a business that is involved in racketeering, can I be held responsible for what they are doing?

If you knowingly invest in any operation or organization that engages in racketeering, you can be prosecuted right along with everyone else in the operation. As an owner or investor, you are expected to ensure the practices are legal, and failing to do that will be very difficult to justify.

36. I know someone who is trying to give people money to start businesses for him. Can the people who start the businesses get in trouble if the guy originally got the money through racketeering?

Yes. The law says a person is prohibited from using funds from racketeering. So the people would be committing a crimes by accepting the money and starting businesses with it.

37. If I were to get a job and participate in racketeering activities at work or invest into a business that is involved in racketeering or use money from racketeering to buy things, how much trouble could I get in if I got caught?

The racketeering charge alone is punishable by imprisonment for up to 20 years and/or a fine of up to $100,000.00. You can also be charged for all of the state's expenses related to investigating, arresting, and convicting you. The state will usually seize all of your money and property and require you to show how they were not relates to the racketeering activities. If you are unable to do so, you will lose them too. [35]

38. Is it illegal to tell someone that they or their family or their property is going to be damaged if they don't surrender some money or do something for you?

Yes. That is extortion, and it is punishable by up to 20 years in prison too. [36]

39. Is it true that you can go to prison for falsely accusing someone of a crime?

Yes. Innocent people have been killed because of malicious accusations. The law now is that anyone who intentionally accuses an innocent person of a crime will themselves be guilty of a felony that is punishable by up to 20 years in prison and/or a fine of up to $10,000.00. [37]

40. What is hazing?

Hazing is a crime that involves subjecting someone to a dangerous activity for the purpose of being accepted into or to remain part of a school organization. [38]

41. Is hazing still a crime if the victim volunteered for it?

Yes. The law says: "It is not a defense [if the] individual against whom the hazing was directed consented to or acquiesced in the hazing." 39

42. Is it still a crime if the person doing the hazing doesn't know it is dangerous?

Yes. The law says: "'Hazing' means an intentional, knowing, or reckless act by a person acting alone or acting with others that is directed against an individual and that the person knew or should have known endangers the physical health or safety to the individual." [40]

43. How much time in jail or prison can someone get for hazing?

If physical injury occurs, hazing is a misdemeanor that carries up to 93 days in jail and/or up to a $1,000.00 fine. If the victim gets severely injured, hazing is a felony that carries up to 5 years and/or up to a $2,500.00 fine. If the victim dies, hazing is a felony that carries up to 15 years and/or up to a $10,000.00 fine. [41]

44. What is a gang felony?

A gang felony is any felony that is committed in relation to one's gang. [42]

45. What does that mean?

It means you can be charged with a major felony if you commit a felony as a gang member or as an associate of a gang. For example, a non-gang member could commit a crime, and they would only be charged with that crime. But as a gang member, you can be charged with the crime and with committing a crime as a gang member or an associate of a gang.

46. How much time does the gang felony carry?

The gang felony alone carries up to 20 years in prison plus however much time you get for the original felony itself. [43]

47. Isn't this double jeopardy?

No. Double jeopardy is convicting you twice for the same crime. The gang felony is not charging you for committing the crime; the gang felony is charging you for being a gang member or associate of a gang while in the commission of a crime.

48. You forgot to tell me what the fine for gang felony is. How much is it?

There is no fine for gang felony. [44] The punishment is incarceration. Society does not want money from gang affiliated criminals. Society wants them locked up.

49. Is it against the law to recruit or encourage someone to join a gang?

Yes. Any attempt to get someone to join a gang is a felony punishable by up to 5 years in prison and/or up to a $5,000.00 fine. [45]

50. Is it a crime to try to keep someone from withdrawing from a gang?

Yes. It is a felony and it carries up to 20 years and/or up to a $20,000.00 fine.

51. What is conspiracy?

Conspiracy is a crime that involves 2 or more people agreeing to commit a crime together. [46]

52. If you get convicted of conspiracy, can you also be convicted of the crime that you conspired to commit?

Yes. If 2 or more people conspire to commit a crime and then commit or attempt to commit it, they can be charged with both the crime and the conspiracy to commit the crime. [47]

53. How is conspiracy punished?

You can be sentenced to the same amount of time in jail or prison for conspiracy to commit a crime as you would get if you actually committed the crime; misdemeanors are limited to up to a $1,000.00 fine, and felonies can only be fined up to $10,000.00.

54. What is solicitation to commit murder?

Any offer to give or do anything for someone else in exchange for their help--in any fashion--to murder or to allow someone to be murdered is solicitation to commit murder. [49]

55. What is the punishment for solicitation to commit murder?

The punishment for solicitation to commit murder is imprisonment for life or any term of years. [50]

56. Is it illegal to solicit or ask someone or bribe someone to commit a crime other than murder?

Yes. Soliciting someone to commit a crime that is punishable with up to 5 years is a misdemeanor punishable by imprisonment for up to 2 years and/or up to a $1,000.00 fine. If the crime is punishable with up to 5 years or more, the solicitation to commit the crime is a felony that is punishable by imprisonment for not more than 5 years and/or not more than a $5,000.00 fine. [51] So that means you can get up to 2 years for trying to talk someone into getting involved in a crime that carries up to 5 or more years.

57. Can you get in more trouble if you solicit a minor?

Yes. Anyone 17 years old or older who "recruits, induces, solicits, or coerces a minor less than 17 years of age to commit or attempt to commit "a felony is guilty of a felony. [52] The punishment for this law is however much time in prison that crime carries. [53] So, for example, if a 17 year old tries to convince a 15 year old to commit a felony that carries up to 5 years in prison, the 17 year old can be sent to prison for up to 5 years for soliciting a minor to commit a felony.

58. If someone attempts to commit murder but does not do it by assaulting someone, like assault with intent to commit murder, what is it called?

Attempted murder. Poisoning, drowning, and strangling are all mentioned in the attempted murder law, but it also says that other means for committing murder also apply. [54] The punishment for attempted murder is imprisonment for life or any number of years. [55]

59. What is the punishment for attempting to commit a crime?

Attempting to commit a crime has a few different punishments. Established in 1931, this law calls for up to 10 years in prison for attempting any crime that if committed would be punishable by the death penalty. You will probably be more interested in the next 2 though. You can get up to 5 years in prison for attempting any crime that if committed calls for 5 years or more in prison. Similarly, you can get up to 2 years in prison or 1 year in jail for attempting any crime that if committed calls for less than 5 years in prison. [56]

Chapter 4

Uttering and Publishing, Forgery, and Counterfeiting

60. What is uttering and publishing?

Uttering means to make something available to people and to put that item into other people's possession. The crime of uttering and publishing then is presenting certain "false, forged, altered, or counterfeit" items as authentic. For example, it is a crime to utter and publish financial transaction devices. [57] That means it is a to forge or counterfeit or alter money or checks or debt cards or other items and pass them off as genuine articles.

61. Is it still called uttering and publishing to forge or counterfeit records or documents of ownership?

Yes. No false or altered document in any commercial, business, contractual, or public exchange may be intentionally passed off as authentic. [58] For example, presenting a fake document to support your claimed to be a licensed builder, registered nurse, or other qualified professional demonstrates one of many ways the uttering and publishing of records and documents of ownership can be illegally used.

62. How much time can you get for uttering and publishing records and other documents?

Not more than 14 years in prison. [59]

64. What does that mean?

To be guilty of uttering and publishing you have to have a false instrument (e.g., an altered receipt, a fake diploma, a forged deed, a counterfeit title), then you have to intend to use it to defraud (i.e., trick) someone for your benefit, and then you have to at least attempt to defraud them. [60]

As complicated as this might sound, all it means is that you try to trick someone into accepting a false document.

65. Is uttering and publishing the same as printing fake money?

No. Forgery of bank bills is the actual printing of counterfeit bills. [61] Uttering and publishing is the passing of those bills into circulation among other people. [62]

66. What is the penalty for forgery of bank bills?

Imprisonment for up to 7 years. [63] This is only the Michigan penalty however. The federal penalty is more likely to apply.

67. What is the punishment for possessing counterfeit notes with the intent to utter them as true?

Possession of counterfeit bills with the intent to use them illegally is a felony punishable by up to 7 years in prison. [64]

68. How much time can I get for passing or using counterfeit money?

The prosecutor can charge you with a number of crimes, including the 14-year uttering and publishing charge mentioned in #62 above. However, the law seems to favor giving a person up to 5 years in prison. [65] As mentioned before you can also get 7 years just for having counterfeit bills and intentions to pass them off as real money.

69. How severe are the penalties for possessing tools or items used in counterfeiting?

The penalties are quite severe: up to 10 years in prison and/or up to a $5,000.00 fine. [66] A single item (e.g., paper, press, computer equipment) is enough to send someone to prison for several years.

Chapter 5

Arson

70. What is first degree arson?

The intentional use of fire or explosives to damage or destroy a multiunit building in which exists at least one dwelling (i.e., a place that could be used as a person's residence), any other building that results in someone getting physically injured, or a mine. [67]

71. What are some examples of first degree arson?

Setting fire to a hotel, motel, dorm, apartment building, nursing home, hospital, resort, bed and breakfast, jail, prison, and any other building that has several components, at least one of which is likely to have someone living in it. Another example of first degree arson is someone getting hurt because they were trying to get away from a burning building that you lit on fire. If anyone gets physically hurt from a fire that you set, the crime immediately becomes first degree arson. [68]

72. What is the punishment for first degree arson?

"[I]imprisonment for life or any term of years or a fine of not more than $20,000.00 or 3 times the value of the property damaged or destroyed, whichever is greater, or both imprisonment and a fine." [69]

73. What happens if someone dies in a fire that I set?

You will be guilty of felony murder (See volume 5.) The punishment is life in prison.

74. If I don't know there is someone in the house and they die, how is that murder? Shouldn't it be considered an accident?

It is felony murder because you intentionally set in motion a force [the fire] likely to cause death or great bodily harm." [70] Once you set the fire, you are totally responsible for it-- even if it goes on to do things that you do not want it to do.

75. If I set a house on fire and the fire spreads to several other houses, can I be charged with more than one count of arson?

Yes. [71] You will most likely be charged with every single building that gets damaged, as well as a number of related charges, especially those that relate to physical injury.

76. Suppose a house is not worth much, has lots of damage, and the owners are not there, would I still be charged with arson?

Yes. The value and condition of the house is irrelevant. The "judge [is] bound to follow [the law which requires the] maximum term for burning a dwelling house irrespective of assessed valuation of the building." [72] The arson sentences are so severe because little kids and babies are often burned to death in fires that people set.

77. Is burning a house first or second degree arson?

Second degree, unless it is part of a multiunit building. [73]

78. What is the main difference between first and second degree arson?

Both deal with arson of dwellings; however, first degree involves multiunit buildings, which have at least one dwelling; whereas second degree involves individual dwellings. [75] So, for example, setting an apartment building on fire would be first degree arson, but setting a house on fire would be second degree arson. However, if anyone (i.e., you, a neighbor, a firefighter, the arson victim, or anyone else) gets injured as a result of the arson, the crime immediately becomes first degree arson. [76] And all arsons of mines are first degree. [77]

79. What is the punishment for second degree arson?

"[I]imprisonment for not more than 20 years or a fine of not more than $20,000.00 or 3 times the value of the property damaged or destroyed, whichever is greater, or both imprisonment and a fine." [78]

80. What is third degree arson?

Maliciously burning buildings and personal property that is valued at $20,000.00 or more. [79]

81. Dwellings are buildings; isn't it third degree arson to burn or blow up a house or other dwelling?

No. First and second degree arson apply to dwellings. Third degree arson applies to other buildings and to personal property worth $20,000.00 or more.

82. If I burn my own property, can I be charged with a crime?

Yes. Arson is not just burning or blowing up other people's property. Some criminals use arson to damage or destroy their own buildings and personal property in hopes of defrauding insurance companies. The law, therefore, prohibits such activities. [80]

83. What is the punishment for third degree arson?

Up to 10 years in prison, a fine of up to $20,000.00 or 3 times the value of the property, or both. [81]

84. What is fourth degree arson?

Fourth degree arson involves using fire or explosives to damage or destroy personal property valued from $1,000.00 to less than $20,000.00. [82] Fourth degree also involves intentionally or negligently setting fire to other people's woods, prairie, or land, or letting fire on your own property spread to other people's property. [83]

85. Do the laws become stricter if you have had a prior arson conviction?

Yes. For instance, fourth degree arson involves property worth at least $1,000.00, but for people with any prior arson convictions the amount is lowered to just $200.00. [84]

86. What is the punishment for fourth degree arson?

Up to 5 years in prison, a fine of up to $10,000.00 or 3 the value of the property, or both. [85]

87. What is arson of insured property?

Arson of insured property is intentionally burning or blowing up insured property with the intent to defraud the insurer. [86]

88. What is the punishment for arson of insured property?

The punishment depends on the circumstances. Arson of insured dwellings carries up to life in prison, a fine of up to $20,000.00 or 3 times the value of the property, or both. Arson of insured buildings and real property carries up to 20 years in prison and/or the fines previously mentioned. Arson of insured personal property carries up to 10 years in prison and/or the fine described above. [87]

89. Does it matter who owns the property?

No. Arson is a crime whether you or someone else owns the property. [88]

90. What is fifth degree arson?

Burning or blowing up personal property valued at up to $1,000.00 or less. This does not include insured property. [89]

91. What is the punishment for fifth degree arson?

This one is a misdemeanor that is punishable by up to 1 year in jail and/or a fine of up to $2,000.00 or 3 times the value of the property. [90]

Notes

1. MCLS 750.349 (1)(a-f)

2. MCLS 750.349 (3)

3. MCLS 750.349b (1)(a-c)

4. id.

5. United States v. Anderson, 608 Fed. Appx. 369, 2015 Fed. App. 0337N, 2015 U.S. App. LEXIS 7691 (6th Cir. Mich.), cert. denied, 136 S. Ct. 264, 2015 U.S. LEXIS 5916 (U.S. 2915).

6. People v. Pratt, 2009 Mich. App. LEXIS 1294 (Mich. Ct. App. June 11, 2009).

7. MCLS 750.349b (2)

8. MCLS 750.411h (1)(d)

9. MCLS 750.411h (2)(a-b)

10. MCLS 750.411h (3)(a-c)

11. MCLS 750.411h (1)(e)(i-vii)

12. MCLS 750.411i (2)(a-d)

13. MCLS 750.411i (3)(a-b)

14. MCLS 750.411i (4)(a-c)

15. MCLS 750.411s (1-2)

16. MCLS 750.411s (6)

17. MCLS 750.167 (1)(a-c, e-l); MCLS 750.168 (1)

18. MCLS 750.167 (1)(d)

19. MCLS 750.168 (2)(a-b)

20. People v. Towlen, 66 Mich. App. 577, 1976 Mich. App. LEXIS 1223 (Mich. Ct. App. 1976).

21. People v. Rea, 38 Mich. App. 141, 1972 Mich. App. LEXIS 1547 ((Mich. Ct. App. 1972).

22. MCLS 750.338b

23. MCLS 750.147b (1)(a-c)

24. MCLS 750.147b (2)

25. MCLS 750.147b (3)(a-b)

26. MCLS 750.543b (a)(i-iii)

27. MCLS 750.543f (2)

28. id.

29. MCLS 750.543k (1-2)

30. MCLS 750.543m (3)

31. MCLS 750.543m (2)

32. MCLS 750.411a (1)(a-e)

33. MCLS 750. 159g (a-rr)

34. MCLS 750.159i (1)

35. MCLS 750.159j

36. MCLS 750.213

37. id.

38. MCLS 750.411t

39. MCLS 750.411t (6)

40. MCLS 750.411t (7)(b)

41. MCLS 750.411t (2)(a-c)

42. MCLS 750.411t (1)

43. MCLS 750.411u (1)

44. id.

45. MCLS 750.411v (1)

46. MCLS 750.157a

47. id.

48. MCLS 750.157a (a-c)

49. MCLS 750.157b (1-2)

50. id.

51. MCLS 750.157b (3)(a-b)

52. MCLS 750.157c

53. id.

54. MCLS 750.91

55. id.

56. MCLS 750.92

57. MCLS 750.248a

58. MCLS 750.249

59. id.

60. People v. Fudge, 66 Mich. App. 625, 1976 Mich. App. LEXIS 1231 (Mich. Ct. App. 1976).

61. MCLS 750.251

62. See supra note 57.

63. See supra note 61.

64. MCLS 750.252

65. MCLS 750. 253

66. MCLS 750. 255

67. MCLS 750.72 (1)(a-c)

68. id.

69. MCLS 750.72 (3)

70. People v. Bonds, 159 Mich. App. 754, 1987 Mich. App. LEXIS 2979 (Mich. Ct. App. 1987).

71. People v. Barber, 255 Mich. App. 288, 2003 Mich. App. LEXIS 286 (Mich. Ct. App. 2003).

72. People v. Losinger, 331 Mich. 490, 1951 Mich. LEXIS 294 (Mich. 1951).

73. MCLS 750.73; See also supra note at 67.

74. See supra note 67.

75. MCLS 750.73

76. MCLS 750.72 (1)(b)

77. MCLS 750.72 (1)(c)

78. MCLS 750.73 (3)

79. MCLS 750.74 (1)(a-b)(i)

80. MCLS 750.74 (2)

81. MCLS 750.74 (3)

82. MCLS 750.75 (1)(a)(i)

83. MCLS 750. 75 (1)(b)

84. MCLS 750.75 (1)(a)(ii)

85. MCLS 750.75 (3)

86. MCLS 750.76 (1)(a-c)

87. MCLS 750. 76 (3)(a-c)

88. MCLS 750.76 (2)

89. MCLS 750.77 (1)

90. MCLS 750.77 (3)

INDEX

Index numbers refer to question numbers, not to page numbers.

abuse (See sexual abuse)

aiding in the commission of a crime: 3, 27, 28, 33

arson:

--fifth degree: 90, 91

--first degree: 70--72, 77, 78, 81

--fourth: 84, 86

--of insured property: 87, 88

--of one's own property: 82

--prior convictions: 85

--second degree: 77-79, 81

--third degree: 80, 81, 83

attempted murder: 58

attempting a crime: 31, 59

beggar: 17

capability: 28

conspiracy: 31, 51-53

counseling or therapy: 10

counterfeiting: 61, 65, 67-69

credible threat: 13, 15

disorderly person: 17

double jeopardy: 47

emotional distress: 8

ethnic intimidation: 20-22

extortion: 38

false reporting of crime: 30, 39

felony:

--felony murder: 73, 74

--gang felony: 44-48

fire department: 25

fleeing a crime: 3

forcing someone to work: 1

forgery: 61, 65, 66

fraud: 31,

free speech: 16

gross indecency: 18, 19

harassment: 7

hazing: 40-43

hostage: 1

indecent or obscene conduct: 17

intent: 28

judicial discretion: 10, 14

juvenile: 9, 14

kidnap: 1-3

loiterer: 17

molest: 1

obscene conduct: (See indecent or obscene conduct)

police: 25

prior convictions: 13, 17

prostitute: 17

public disturbance: 17

pushing people: 17

race: 20

racketeering: 31, 32, 34-37

ransom: 1

rape: 1

reasonable person: 15

school: 25

secretly confined: 3

sexual abuse: 1

sexual delinquent: 19

social media: 15

solicitation of a minor: 57

solicitation to commit a crime: 56

solicitation to commit murder: 54, 55

stalking:

--aggravated: 13-15

--generally: 7-12

terrorism: 23-29

therapy (See counseling and therapy)

threat: 20

threatening to commit a crime: 29

unlawful imprisonment: 3-6

uttering and publishing: 61-65

vagrant: 17

weapon: 3, 5

window peeper: 17

10.

Prostitution and Human Trafficking

Chapter 1 Prostitution 271

Chapter 2 Pandering 275

Chapter 3 House of Prostitution 283

Notes 285

Index 287

CHAPTER 1

PROSTITUTION

1. What is prostitution?

Prostitution is exchanging sexual acts for money, goods, or services.

2. Is prostitution illegal?

Yes. [1]

3. What are some examples of soliciting?

Accosting, soliciting, and inviting some one to commit prostitution are all illegal. [2] Accosting is approaching a person. Soliciting is enticing them to engage in sex for money. Inviting is welcoming someone to participate in prostitution. So, respectively, examples could be walking up to someone in effort to give them sex for money or trying to persuade someone to participate in prostitution with you or offering to perform sexual activities with someone in exchange for money. [3]

4. If an 18 year old adult offers sex for money or favors, is the penalty the same?

Yes, but the prostitution law applies to people who are 16 years old or older. So if a 16 year old offers sex for money or favors, the 16 year old can be prosecuted too. [4]

5. What is the penalty for soliciting, accosting, or inviting someone to commit prostitution or immoral acts?

Unless otherwise stated, the penalty is a misdemeanor punishable by up to 93 days in jail and/or up to a $5,000.00 fine. If the person has a prior conviction of this sort, the second offense is punishable by up to 1 year in jail and/or up to a $1,000.00 fine. If the person has 2 or more prior convictions of this sort, the third and subsequent offenses are punishable by up to 2 years of incarceration and/or up to a $2,000.00 fine. [5] These punishments are what the prostitute receives.

6. What is the penalty for someone who engages in sex for money with a prostitute who is under 18 years old?

Imprisonment for up to 5 years and/or up to a $10,000.00 fine. [6] If someone pays someone who is under 18 years old for sex, that person faces up to 5 years in prison; however, this is an extremely sensitive issue that could easily turn into a criminal sexual conduct (e.g., rape) case, depending on the age of the prostitute/victim.

7. The penalty for an adult who pays a prostitute for sex is up to 93 days in jail and it gets more severe with repeated offenses?

Yes. [7]

8. If I helped a prostitute or a person in search of a prostitute to commit prostitution, would that be a crime?

Yes. [8] Regardless of whether you assisted them a little or a lot, if you help someone to commit prostitution, you are guilty of a crime that might be a misdemeanor or a felony, depending on the circumstances involved.

Chapter 2

Pandering

9. Suppose I want to earn a living off of prostitutes. Is that illegal?

The law says "Any person who knowingly accepts, receives, levies, or appropriates any money or valuable thing [from] any person engaged in prostitution, or any person...who lives or derives support or maintenance, in whole or in part, from the earnings or proceeds of the prostitution of a prostitute...is guilty of a felony punishable by imprisonment for not more than 20 years." [9]

10. Why is the law so strict on the people who manage prostitutes?

"Managing" makes it sound legal, but the 20 year sentence reflects the dangers and damages that such managers pose to prostitutes and the public.

11. Is there a law against charging prostitutes to protect them, provide them food and shelter, buy them clothes, bond them out of jail, take

them to the doctor, find them safe customers, and other such needs that they might have?

The law is clear: it is illegal to accept money or valuables from a prostitute if you are any form of a"keeper or manager" for them. [10] The penalty is up to 20 years in prison.

12. How could anyone ever know whether I am managing prostitutes?

Prostitutes are people, and people sometimes get angry or desperate. When people are angry or desperate, they sometimes do things that they would not ordinarily do, such as telling the police what you have been doing.

13. If they are prostitutes, how can their testimony be any stronger than mine?

"In prosecution for accepting money from earnings of prostitite, evidence was sufficient to sustain conviction, although prosecution was forced to rely on witnesses who were not of the best character and in whose testimony there were inconsistencies." [11] This case shows that the prosecution does not have to have an air tight case to convict someone.

In fact, the prosecutor does not even need more than one person to testify against you. In People v. Costanza a "self-confessed prostitute" testified that the defendant took her to engage in prostitution. She then testified that she gave the defendant half of the money. The jury believed her, and the defendant was found guilty of accepting money from the earnings of a prostitute. [12] Law does not require absolute proof to get a conviction. All the prosecutor has to do is convince a jury that you probably committed the crime.

Another case that demonstrates how easily one might get convicted is People v. Podsiad. [13] In this case the defendant rented a room in his basement to a woman who then engaged in prostitution there. The defendant claimed he did not know about her activities. He claimed the money she gave him was for room and board. The jury did not believe him and he was found guilty of accepting money from the earnings of a prostitute.

14. Is it true that transporting prostitutes from one state to another is punishable by up to 20 years?

The federal law is outside the scope of this publication, but it is true that transporting someone "through or across this state...for the purpose of prostitution or with the intent and purpose to induce, entice or compel that person to become a prostitute is [] a felony, punishable by imprisonment for not more than 20 years." [14]

15. Why is transporting prostitutes across the state so bad?

Though you might not see it, many people's lives are ruined due to being trapped by other people who force them to become proatitutes. For someone who would resist, maybe even if it killed them, this concept might be difficult to imagine. However, people--often children--are forced daily into lifestyles such as prostitution, and these laws are intended to severely punish the people who try to trap them into such dangerous lifestyles and activities.

16. How do people attempt to trap people in prostitution?

The law does not describe the exact methods, but it does state what is illegal. For instance, it is a crime, punishable by up to 20 years in prison, to do any of the following: get someone to live or work in a house of prostitution, persuade someone to become a prostitute, force or trick someone into engaging in prostitution, coax someone into this state or out of this state for the purpose of prostitution, or giving or receiving money or valuables to turn someone onto a prostitute. [15]

17. What is forced labor or services?

Forced labor is like slavery. It is forcing people to work without giving them wages or compensation. This is not sex related though. [16]

18. What is holding an individual in debt bondage?

Debt bondage is forcing someone to work for you because they owe you for something but refusing to reduce their debt in fair exchange for their labor. [17] For example, you might allow someone to live at your house for free for a while, and then you might force them to clean your house everyday for the rest of your life because they owe you. That is debt bondage because you are not allowing the person to identify (1) how much they owe you and (2) how much they are earning by cleaning your house. In that scenario the clwaner cannot determine how long it will take to pay off the debt.

19. Is it illegal to recruit or acquire people to do forced labor or services or debt bondage for other people?

Yes. Whether you are forcing people to work for you and/or holding people in debt bondage or getting people for others to force to work and/or hold in debt bondage, you are committing a serious crime. [18]

20. What is the punishment for recruiting or acquiring people for forced labor or debt bondage?

The punishment is the same for recruiting as it is for actually holding a person in forced labor pr debt bondage, which is up to 10 years and/or up to a $10,000.00 fine. If the victim gets physically injured, the punishment increases to up to 15 years in prison and/or up to a $15,000.00 fine. If the injury is serious, the punishment increases to up to 20 years and/or up to a $20,000.00 fine. And if the crime "involves kidnapping or attempted kidnapping, criminal sexual conduct" or other similarly serious crimes, the punishment increases to life or any term of years and/or a fine of up to $50,000.00. [19]

21. Is the punishment different between people who hold others in forced labor or debt bondage and people who merely try to or conspire to?

"A person who attempts, conspires, or solicits another to [hold someone in forced labor or debt bondage] is subject to the same penalty as a person who commits [the crime]." [20

Chapter 3

House of Prostitution

22. What is a house of prostitution?

The law has several names for them such as "house of ill-fame, bawdy house," and such, but a house of prostitution is basically any structure out of which prostitutes work.

23. Is it against the law to operate a house of prostitution?

Yes. Keeping, operating, maintaining, or supporting the operation of a house of prostitution is a felony that is punishable by up to 5 years in prison and/or up to a $5,000.00 fine. [21]

24. What is the difference between accepting money from the earnings of a prostitute and operating a house of prostitution?

The main differences involve (1) punishment and (2) relation to the prostitute. The punishment for accepting money from the earnings of a prostitute is up to 20 years in prison; however, the punishment for operating a house of prostitution is up to 5 years in prison. The difference between these punishments is so large because the relation between the prostitute and the other party is radically different. The person who receives money from the prostitute's earnings is a manager (i.e., a pimp), which the law identifies as largely being responsible for the prostitute engaging in prostitution. On the other hand, the person who operates a house of prostitution is not controlling the prostitute or necessarily responsible for the prostitute choosing to engage in prostitution.

25. Can I get in trouble for working at the door to a house of prostitution?

Yes. The law says, "A person...who receives or admits...a person into a place, structure, house, building, or vehicle for the purpose of prostitution...is guilty of a crime punishable [as stated in the answer to question #5 above.] [22]

26. If a prostitute runs up a debt in a house of prostitution and you attempt to detain the prostitute until the debt is paid, can you go to prison for that?

Yes. No one has the right to stop someone else from leaving a house of prostitution. Anyone who attempts to stop someone else from leaving "is guilty of a felony punishable by imprisonment for not less than 2 years or more than 20 years." [23]

NOTES

1. MCLS 750.448

2. id.

3. id.

4. id.

5. MCLS 750.451 (1-3)

6. MCLS 750.451 (4)

7. See supra note 5.

8. MCLS 750.450

9. MCLS 750.457

10. id.

11. People v. Southern, 306 Mich. 324, 1943 Mich. LEXIS 617 (Mich. 1943).

12. People v. Costanza, 306 Mich. 415, 1943 Mich. LEXIS 628 (Mich. 1943).

13. People v. Podsiad, 295 Mich 541, 1940 Mich. LEXIS 682 (Mich. 1940).

14. MCLS 750.459

15. MCLS 750.455 (a-h)

16. MCLS 750.462a (g)

17. MCLS 750.462a (d)

18. MCLS 750.462d

19. MCLS 750.462f (1)(a-d)

20. MCLS 750.462f (3)

21. MCLS 750. 452

22. See supra note 5.

23. MCLS 750.458

INDEX

Index numbers refer to question numbers, not to page numbers.

accost: 3, 5

attempts: 21

claiming ignorance: 13

criminal sexual conduct: 6, 20

debt bondage: 18-20

favors: 4

forced labor: 17, 19, 20

house of prostitution: 22-26

immoral acts: 5

invite: 3, 5

kidnapping: 20

--attempted: 20

pandering/managing prostitutes: 9-12, 24

prior convictions: 5, 7

prostitution: 1-16, 22, 24, 26

rape: 6

solicit: 3, 5, 21

transporting prostitutes: 14, 15

under 18 years old: 6

11.

Rape and Criminal Sexual Conduct

Chapter 1 CSC--First Degree and Third Degree..291

Chapter 2 CSC--Second Degree and Fourth Degree 297

Chapter 3 Assault w/Intent, Testimony, Resistance, DNA, Monitoring 303

Notes 307

Index 309

Chapter 1

CSC--First Degree and Third Degree

1. What is criminal sexual conduct--first degree?

First degree criminal sexual conduct (CSC) is the modern term for rape. CSC has four classifications; CSC in the first and third degree occurs when a person "engages in sexual penetration with another person" in violation of certain parts of the law. [1]

2. What is sexual penetration?

"Sexual penetration means sexual intercourse, [touching one's mouth to another's genitals], anal intercourse, or any intrusion, however slight, of any part of a person's body or of any object into the genital or anal openings of another's body, but emission of semen is not required." [2]

3. So the first and third degrees of CSC involve sexual penetration?

Yes.

4. What are some of the differences between first and third degree CSC?

First degree CSC is the more severe of the two crimes. If the victim is under 13 years old, the CSC is automatically first degree. [3]

5. What if both of the people are only 12 years old?

"The age of the offender is not a relevant concern; there is no public policy that prohibits [charging] an offender who is also in the same age range at the time the offense was committed." [4] This quote is from a Michigan CSC case where the victim and offender were young minors--not 12--but young enough for there to be significant concern whether they were too young to be charged. The point here is that the law even applies too especially young adolescent offenders.

6. Can first degree CSC occur if the victim is 13 or older?

If the victim is 13, 14, or 15, the CSC is first degree if the offender is a member of the same household, related by blood or by marriage, in a position of authority (e.g., a teacher), working for a school system, or working with a child care organization or foster care home or group. [5] This is an especially dangerous area for young teenagers who move into a foster home and fall in love rather than bond as foster siblings.

7. Are there any other ways to turn a CSC into first degree?

Yes. If the penetration occurs while the offender is committing another felony (e.g., home invasion), if the offender is armed, if the offender injures the victim--which also means getting them pregnant-- and if the offender is assisted in the crime by anyone else and the offender knows the victim is mentally incapable, mentally incapacitated, or physically helpless. [6] Mentally incapable means mentally challenged to the point that they cannot give you consent to have sex with them. [7] Mentally incapacitated means mentally unable to judge or control one's conduct due to someone else giving them drugs or alcohol without their consent. [8] Former example, putting drugs in someone's drink to make them easier to have sex with is first degree CSC if you do it and then have sex with them. Physically helpless means unconscious. [9] That means, for example, having sex with a person who is passed out drunk is first degree CSC.

8. What is the punishment for first degree CSC?

First degree CSC is "punishable by imprisonment for life or any term of years." [10] If the offender is at least 17 years old and the victim is less than 13 years old, the offender must be sentenced to serve no less than 25 years in prison. [11] If the offender has a prior CSC conviction, they are at least 18 years old, and the victim is under 13, the punishment is imprisonment for life without the possibility of parole. [12] Also, the law requires offenders who have been convicted of first degree CSC to submit to lifetime electronic monitoring if they are ever released from prison.

9. How is third degree CSC different from first degree CSC?

Third degree CSC applies if the victim is 13, 14, or 15 years old. [13] Third degree also applies if force or coercion is used; if the offender knows the victim is mentally incapable, mentally incapacitated, or physically helpless; if the offender and victim are related by blood or by marriage; if the offender works for a school system and the victim is 16 or 17 years old; if the offender works for a school system and the victim is 16-25 years old and receiving special education services; or if the offender is working with a child care organization or foster care home or group. [14]

10. What is the punishment for third degree CSC?

Third degree CSC is punishable by not more than 15 years in prison. [15]

11. Suppose someone put a drug in someone's drink and waited for them to pass-out and then had sex with them and then got caught or maybe they just got accused of the crime. Can the prosecutor charge them with more than one count of CSC?

Yes. [16] Each charge represents a different law. For example, in MCL 750.520b (1)(c), which is part of the first degree CSC law, we can read that it can be apply when "sexual penetration occurs [during] the commission of any other felony." So drugging someone would be a felony and the sexual penetration afterward would make the crime first degree CSC. However, MCL 750.520d (1)(c), which is part of the third degree CSC law, tells us CSC-III occurs when "the actor knows or has reason to know that the victim is mentally incapable, mentally incapacitated, or physically helpless." So the sexual penetration with a passed-out person would make the crime third degree CSC, too.

Chapter 2
CSC--Second Degree and Fourth Degree

12. What is CSC in the second degree?

Second degree CSC is illegal sexual contact (i.e., unwanted touching of a victim's sexual parts--above or below clothing--for sexual malicious purposes [17]) when any of the following apply: (1) the victim is under 13 years old; (2) the victim is 13-15 years old and living in the same household as the offender or they are related or the offender is in a position of authority over the victim or the offender is a teacher or working for the school system or a child care organization; (3) the sexual contact occurs during the commission of a felony; (4) the offender is assisted by someone else and knows the victim is unable to resist or understand the nature of the sexual contact or the offender uses force or coercion; (5) the offender is armed or the offender has something that the victim believes to be a weapon; (6) the offender injures the victim; (7) the victim is a relative or subordinate and mentally incapable, incapacitated, or helpless; or (8) the victim is a prisoner or probationer and the offender works for the state or a company that provides services to the state. [18]

13. That is too complicated; what is second degree CSC?

CSC is illegal sexual contact, not penetration, but serious nevertheless.

14. What is the punishment for CSC second degree?

Imprisonment for up to 15 years. Also, if the offender is 17 years or older and the victim is 12 or younger, the offender must submit to lifetime electronic monitoring if they ever get out of prison. [19]

15. Suppose a teenage girl's mother marries a teenage boy's father. The teens are not related by blood and as soon as they meet they fall in love. Can they get in trouble for having sexual contact?

Yes. (See answer to question #6) By law, stepbrothers and stepsisters are prohibited from having sexual contact with one another. [20] For teens who are in love and in the same family via marriage--not blood--the dilemma might seem hopeless; however, the law is in place to provide the young people an opportunity to bond as siblings rather than as spouses. Later, after the teens legally move out of their parents' home and are of age to make their own decisions, the law no longer restricts step-siblings from sexual contact as long as they are not related by blood. However, if the teens have sexual contact prior to both of them coming of age and living outside of their parents' (or other caregivers') home, the teens will be guilty of second degree CSC, and they can be sent to prison as sexual offenders.

16. Is it automatically second degree CSC if someone has sexual contact with someone under 13 years old?

Yes. [21]

17. What if the offender is under 13 too?

Age does not excuse this crime. If a person has sexual contact with a child, it is a sex crime: second degree CSC. [22]

18. What is the age of consent?

The age of consent is the age when a person can legally choose whether or not to engage in sexual activity. [23] In Michigan the age of consent is 16 years old. This means people are entirely prohibited from having sexual contact with people under 16 years old.

19. Is it still CSC if, for example, your girlfriend is 15 and she knows all about sex and she agrees to have sex AND her parents permit her to be sexually active?

The parents do not have the authority to give their daughter permission to break the law. It is against the law for anyone to have sexual contact with anyone under 16 years old. This is one of the laws that puts young teenagers in a bad situation if they get caught because the teens do not usually realize they are committing a sex crime that will go on their record, and they will face going to an institution e.g., jail, prison, juvenile detention), rather than college, the military, or the work force.

20. What is fourth degree CSC?

Fourth degree CSC is illegal contact that is less severe than second degree. For example, second degree CSC begins by prohibiting sexual contact with children under 13 years old; but fourth degree CSC begins by prohibiting sexual contact between people who are 13-15 years old and offenders who are 5 or more years older than them. Fourth degree CSC also applies to sexual contact between people who could otherwise consent to sexual contact if they wanted to, so other instances of CSC-IV include using force or coercion to make sexual contact, making sexual contact when the victim cannon resist or understand the activity, having sexual contact with family members--whether by blood or marriage--and having sexual contact with certainly people (e.g., one's studenta or patient). [24]

21. What is the punishment for fourth degree CSC?

Fourth degree CSC is a misdemeanor punishable by up to 2 years in jail or prison or up to a $500.00 fine, or both. [25] Fourth degree CSC is a special kind of misdemeanor that allows the judge to send someone to prison or jail for longer than most misdemeanor call for. More importantly though, fourth degree CSC is very similar to second degree CSC, which means people who commit fourth degree CSC could also face charges for second degree CSC--a crime that could send them to prison for up to 15 years.

22. Is it true that the judge has to give you a certain amount of time if you are a second time offender?

Sort of. The law calls for a "mandatory minimum sentence of at least 5 years" for sexual offenders who reoffend. [26] That means the judge can give you more time but not less than 5 years, regardless of the circumstances of the case.

Chapter 3

Assault w/Intent, Testimony, Resistance, DNA, Monitoring

23. What is assault with intent to commit CSC?

This is a crime that has 2 categories (i.e., sexual penetration and sexual contact). Assault with intent to commit CSC involving penetration is a felony punishable by up to 10 years in prison. The crime itself involves an assault and an intent to commit CSC first or third degree (i.e., penetration). [27] For example, in the attempt to commit CSC, an offender might hit a victim just before the victim escapes or is rescued. Though the offender did not succeed in raping the victim, the offender will be sentenced to up to 10 years for the assault and intent. The next category is assault with intent to commit CSC in the second degree, which is a felony punishable by up to 5 years in prison. The crime involves an assault and an intent to commit CSC second degree (i.e., sexual contact). [28] For example, an offender, who is captured after assaulting but before molesting the victim, would be guilty of this crime.

24. If it is my word against my victim's word, can I be found guilty of a sex crime?

Yes. The law states, "The testimony of a victim need not be corroborates (i.e., supported by other evidence) in prosecutions under sections 520b to 520g [which are the CSC laws]. [29]

25. What if someone lies and says you raped them and you really didn't do it?

It is a very serious crime to falsely accuse someone of a crime, but aside from that, it would be up to the prosecutor to decide whether to charge you, up to the judge to decide whether to dismiss the case, and up to a jury to decide whether to convict you. Nevertheless, your concern over being wrongfully accused is reasonable.

26. If I go to make sexual contact with someone and they don't resist, does that mean they consent?

No. The law specifically states, "A victim need not resist the actor in prosecution under section 520b to 520g [which are the CSC laws]." [30] This means no one has a right to make sexual contact with anyone else. Everyone has the right to be unmolested, and by law, no one has to tell anyone "no" or "I don't want you to touch me that way." Therefore, people who engage in sexual contact need to be absolutely certain they have the other person's consent.

27. How does the state get people's DNA?

DNA is taken when people are arrested for felonies and for some misdemeanors. [31]

28. What is lifetime electronic monitoring?

Lifetime electronic monitoring is a requirement that Michigan has for all first and second degree CSC offenders who get out of prison. [32] It means these ex-offenders, if released from prison, will have an electronic tracking device attached to them for the rest of their lives. Tampering with or removing the device is a felony.

Notes

1. MCLS 750.520b (1)

2. People v. Harris, 158 Mich. App. 463, 1987 Mich. App. LEXIS 2322 (Mich. Ct. App. 1987).

3. See supra note 1; People v. Favors, 121 Mich. App. 98, 1982 Mich. App. LEXIS 3621 (Mich. Ct. App. 1982).

4. In re Hildebrant, 216 Mich. App. 384, 1996 Mich. App. LEXIS 117 (Mich. Ct. App. 1996).

5. MCLS 750.520b (1)(b)(i-vi)

6. MCLS 750.520b (1)(c-h)

7. MCLS 750.520a (j)

8. MCLS 750. 520a (k)

9. MCLS 750.520a (m)

10. MCLS 750. 520b (2)(a)

11. MCLS 750.520b (2)(b)

12. MCLS 750.520b (2)(c)

13. MCLS 750.520d (1)(a)

14. MCLS 750.520d (1)(b-g)

15. MCLS 750.520d (2)

16. People v. Garland, 286 Mich. App. 1, 2009 Mich. App. LEXIS 2124 (Mich. Ct. App. 2009).

17. MCLS 750.520a (q)

18. MCLS 750.520c (1)

19. MCLS 750. 520c (2)(a-b)

20. People v. Armstrong, 212 Mich. App. 121, 1995 Mich. App. LEXIS 338 (Mich. Ct. App. 1995).

21. People v. Favors, 121 Mich. App. 98, 1982 Mich. App. LEXIS 3621 (Mich. Ct. App. 1982).

22. See supra note 4.

23. MCLS 750.520b, MCLS 750.520c, MCLS 750.520d, People v. Martz, 301 Mich. App. 247, 2013 Mich. App. LEXIS 963 (Mich. Ct. App. 2013).

24. MCLS 750.520e (1)(a-h)

25. MCLS 750.520e (2)

26. MCLS 750.520f (1-2)

27. MCLS 750.520g (1)

28. MCLS 750.520h (2)

29. MCLS 750.520h

30. MCLS 750.520i

31. MCLS 750.520m (1)(a-b)

32. MCLS 750. 520n (1)

INDEX

Index numbers refer to question numbers, not to page numbers.

"age of consent": 18

assault with intent to commit CSC

--first degree: 23

--second degree: 23

--third degree: 23

coercion: (See force or coerce)

criminal sexual conduct (CSC)

--assisted by someone else: 12

--during commission of another crime: 11, 12

--first degree: 1, 3, 4, 6-9, 11, 28 (See also sexual penetration)

--fourth degree: 20, 21

--mentally incapable: 9, 11

--mentally incapacitated: 9, 11

--physically helpless: 9, 11

--related by blood or marriage: 9, 15

--second degree: 12-17, 20, 21, 28 (See also sexual contact)

--third degree: 1, 3, 4, 9-11 (See also sexual penetration)

--working for a school system: 9

--working with a childcare organization: 9

--working with a foster care home or group: 9

DNA: 27

drugging someone: 7, 11

force or coerce: 9, 12, 20

lifetime electronic monitoring: 8, 14, 28

mandatory minimum sentence: 8, 22

multiple charges: 11

offender

--17 years old or older: 14

--armed: 12

--assisted by someone: 12

--in a position of authority: 6, 12, 20

--member of household (with victim): 6, 12, 15

--related by blood or marriage: 6, 9

--under 13 years old: 5, 17

--working for a school system: 6, 9, 12

--working with a childcare organization: 6, 9, 12

--working with a fostercare home or group: 6, 9, 12

--word against the victim's word: 24, 25

penetration (See sexual penetration)

prior convictions: 8, 22

rape: 1, 23, 25 (See also criminal sexual conduct)

sexual activity: 18

sexual contact: 12, 13, 15, 16, 19, 20, 26 (See also criminal sexual conduct)

--assisted by someone: 12

--injuring victim: 12

--not penetration: 13

--position of authority: 12, 20

--same household: 12, 15, 20

--victim is mentally incapable: 12

--victim is mentally incapacitated: 12

--victim is physically helpless: 12

--victim is under 13 years old: 16

--while armed: 12

--while committing another crime: 12

--working for a school system: 12

--working with a childcare organization: 12

sexual penetration (See also criminal sexual conduct)

--during commission of another crime: 7, 11, 12

--impregnating the victim: 7

--injuring victim: 7

--victim is mentally incapable: 7, 9, 11

--victim is mentally incapacitated: 7, 9, 11

--victim is physically helpless: 7, 9, 11

--while armed: 7

victim

--13, 14, or 15 years old: 6, 9, 12, 18-20

--16 or 17 years old: 9

--is a relative: 6, 9, 12, 15, 20

--offender's word against victim's word: 24, 25

--receiving special education services: 9

--unable to resist or understand: 12, 20

--under 13 years old: 4, 5, 8, 12, 14, 16, 20

12.

Robbery

Chapter 1 Unarmed Robbery 315

Chapter 2 Armed Robbery 319

Chapter 3 Carjacking 327

Chapter 4 Bank, Safe, or Vault Robbery 331

Notes 335

Index 339

Chapter 1

Unarmed Robbery

1. What is unarmed robbery?

Unarmed robbery is using "force or violence against any person [or] assault[ing] or put[ting a] person in fear" while committing a larceny of money or property. [1]

2. How much time in prison can you get for unarmed robbery?

Up to 15 years. [2]

3. If I use force or put someone in fear during an attempt to get away after a crime, does that count?

Yes. Using force or fear before, during, or after the larceny (i.e., the theft) is enough to turn the incident into unarmed robbery. [3]

4. So, if I shove someone and take something from him or her, I am committing unarmed robbery?

Yes. To convict you of unarmed robbery, the prosecutor only has to show that you illegally took something by "force and violence, assault or putting in fear" while not being armed. [4]

5. If no one gets hurt, how can it be a robbery case?

Whether someone gets hurt is irrelevant. The penalty might get worse if someone gets hurt, but the crime is committed as soon as you take someone's money or property by force or fear. To see this principle demonstrated in a real case, consider the defendant in People v. Hicks. He grabbed a lady's purse, but she was temporarily able to hold onto it before he snatched it away from her. The force that he used to pull the purse away from her was enough to establish that force was used, and Hicks was convicted of unarmed robbery. [5]

6. What is another example of unarmed robbery?

The victim, in People v. Hudson, got into a fight and some money was taken from him. [6] The fight itself might have resulted in some jail time, but the thoughtless act of taking some of the victim's money turned a fight into a robbery. In a similar case the defendant noticed his wallet missing after two men assaulted him as he exited a saloon. [7] In both cases the defendants threw away years of their lives for a few dollars and some cheap thrills. These are common enough occurrences, so juries find people guilty without overwhelming evidence; for example, in People v. Hipshire the victim was robbed by a group of people. The victim and the witnesses could not be certain whether the defendant actually took anything from him, but the defendant had been overheard planning to rob the victim, and the defendant was in the group that did actually rob the victim. So the jury found him guilty. [8]

7. What is an example of the "force" that is needed to convict someone of unarmed robbery?

The force can be something directly affecting the person such as "twisting [the] victim's arm and taking her purse," as we see in People v. Williams. [9] Or the force can be the mere "tug on the purse strap," as seen in People v. Hicks. [10] Force can even be demonstrated in the defendant's escape attempt where he tries to wrestle himself free without "directing force or violence at any person" in particular. [11]

8. So if I try to steal from a store and their security grabs me and I struggle with them, can I be charged with unarmed robbery instead of retail fraud?

Yes. [12] The retail fraud is the theft, but it becomes unarmed robbery if you use force or fear at any time leadind up to, during, or leaving the crime. [13]

9. Is it unarmed robbery if I intimidate someone into giving me their money?

In People v. Laker the defendant walked into a diner early in the morning when only a waitress was there. The defendant had his hand in his pockets, and all he did was tell the waitress to hand him the money and to lie on the floor. The waitress initially thought he was playing a joke on her, but when she realized he was serious, she became scared and gave him the money. This actual crime is an example of someone using fear instead of force to commit an unarmed robbery. [14]

Chapter 2

Armed Robbery

10. What is armed robbery?

Armed robbery is (1) assaulting someone, (2) taking property from them, and (3) possessing a dangerous weapon. [15]

11. What is the punishment for armed robbery?

Imprisonment for life or any term of years. [16]

12. What is an example of armed robbery?

In People v. Halliburton the defendant pushed a lady to the ground, took her purse, and hit her companion with a 3-foot stick. [17] Here we find two assaults (i.e., pushing the lady and hitting the companion), the larceny of the purse, and the dangerous weapon.

13. If one person, with a firearm, robs five people at once, is that one robbery or five robberies?

The prosecutor can treat it in either way, but technically it is five robberies in one continuous chain of events. [18]

14. Why is robbery even a law?

The legislators want to deter people from threatening and injuring others when the criminals are trying to take money and property from people. [19] Robbery is the law that accomplishes that deterrence.

15. Is it robbery if you lock someone in a room and then steal their property?

In People v. McCray the defendant, at gunpoint, locked the victim, a clerk of a cleaning establishment, in a bathroom, and then stole the victim's purse and money from the cash register. [20] This case demonstrates armed robbery in a way that could easily be overlooked or misunderstood: the victim does not have to be physically in possession of the money or property that is being stolen.

16. If a store clerk does not own the money that I take from the cash register during the robbery, how can I be charged with robbery at all?

In People v. Jones we find that actual ownership of property is not necessary in a robbery case, as long as the victim's right to possession of the property is greater than the defendant's right to possession. [21]

So although the clerk does not actually own the money in the cash register, the clerk has more right to possess it than you do. In People v. Needham we find that the larceny element of robbery is satisfied when property belonging to anyone other than the robber is taken. [22] This means that any stealing that occurs when force or fear are used is robbery. The ownership issue is not accepted in court if the property does not belong to the robber.

17. If I do something that someone else gets scared by, I can't help it if they give me their money. Is it my fault if someone gets scared?

In People v. Kruper we find that "threat to do injury...causing property or money to be given up...can constitute robbery...regardless of how slight the...cause creating the fear may be." [23] This means words and actions that you believe are insignificant could later be used against you if someone says those words or actions are why they gave you their money or property. A great way to protect yourself from being charged with robbery is to avoid threatening people, demanding money or property that is not yours, and accepting money or property that is not yours.

18. Is it robbery to demand money from people by threatening to harm NOT them but someone else who you do not take anything from?

Yes. In People v. Lawson the defendant was found guilty of armed robbery for holding a gun to one customer's head while he took property from the other customers of the store. [24] The fear in this case was that he would kill the customer. That fear is one of the elements of robbery; it can be fear or force but one of the elements have to be present in one manner or another. [25]

19. If I only hint that I might be angry or not like it if they don't give me what I want, can I still be prosecuted for robbery?

If you say or do anything "regardless of how slight" that gives a person "reasonable belief that he may suffer injury unless he complies with the demand," you are setting yourself up to be charged with robbery. If you have a dangerous weapon, you will face armed robbery charges; if not, unarmed robbery.

20. If I don't accept the money or property, I can't be convicted of robbery. Is that correct?

No, that is incorrect. If you make someone move money or goods against their will, you have indirectly taken possession of the money or goods by asportation. [26] That means the person that moved the money or property was acting in your place.

21. If you rob someone for something, maybe you had a good reason for doing it. Could that be a good defense?

The circumstances of the crime help indicate the intent of the perpetrator. In People v. Fisk the perpetrator got intoxicated, masked his face, and warned the gas station attendant not to call the police. [27] Without anything to suggest otherwise, a reasonable person would interpret Fisk's actions as indications of his intent to rob the gas station. If someone has a good reason to commit a crime, they should discuss it with the authorities and a good lawyer before doing so.

22. If I tell someone to give me their money, is that armed robbery if they later say, "I thought he had a weapon"?

If the victim assumes that you must be armed--even though you have not indicated such nor has the victim seen a weapon--the victim's assumptions alone are not enough to satisfy the possession of a dangerous weapon requirement of armed robbery. [28]

23. So, to convict someone of armed robbery, the victim must see the weapon?

No, that is incorrect. If the defendant is engaged in what would otherwise be unarmed robbery and the defendant does any of the following actions, the defendant is guilty of armed robbery: (1) possesses a dangerous weapon or (2) possesses something else that a reasonable person would regard as a dangerous weapon or (3) says that he has a dangerous weapon or (4) indicates that he has a dangerous weapon. [29]

24. So if I put my hand in my sweatshirt pocket and point my finger at someone, as if it is a gun, and demand money, I can be convicted of armed robbery?

If the victim responds by giving you money, yes, that is armed robbery because you indicated that you had a dangerous weapon. By doing that, you would be putting the victim in fear, and that is what the lawmakers made the robbery laws to prevent: people using force or fear to steal money or property. So, yes, you can be convicted of armed robbery if you use a "finger gun" to induce fear during a robbery. [30]

25. Okay, I don't want to commit a robbery anyway, but I sometimes like to plan them. Can I get in trouble if someone commits a robbery that I planned?

Yes. If you encourage, counsel, or assist another in the commission of an armed robbery, you are guilty of being an aider and abettor to armed robbery. (31) According to People v. Hogan, the person who plans a robbery can be convicted as the main participant, even if the planner never participates in the actual robbery. [32] Whether you plan the robbery, carry the gun, run away with the money, or drive the getaway car, you are participating in armed robbery. People v. Loncar tells us joining plans to rob someone makes one guilty of robbery if the robbery occurs. [33]

Chapter 3

Carjacking

26. What is carjacking?

Carjacking is using force or fear, or the threat of violence, to steal someone's vehicle. [34]

27. Does it matter whether you use a weapon during the carjacking?

The crime is carjacking whether you use a weapon or not. In People v. Parker the defendant used a gun to rob the victim of an automobile and money. The defendant was convicted of carjacking for taking the automobile and armed robbery for taking the money. [35]

28. Why wouldn't they both be armed robbery?

The Michigan legislators wanted a law to specifically target criminals who rob people of their automobiles. Carjacking is the law that the legislators enacted. Under this law, robbing someone of their automobile is called carjacking.

29. How much time in jail or prison can you get for carjacking?

Carjacking is "a felony punishable by imprisonment for life or any term of years." [36]

30. Does carjacking and armed robbery have the same potential sentence?

Yes. You can get up to life in prison for committing either crime. [37]

31. Does carjacking and unarmed robbery have the same potential sentence?

No. Carjacking is punishable by up to life in prison; whereas, unarmed robbery is punishable by up to 15 years in prison. [38]

32. If I take someone's car and phone from them, without using a weapon, how much time can I get?

Up to life for the car and up to 15 years for the phone.

33. Suppose the judge gives me 10 years for the carjacking and 5 years for the unarmed robbery of the phone, are the sentences blended together so the 5 years is served while I am serving the 10 years, or are they stacked so I will have to finish serving one before I can start serving the other one?

That is up to the judge. The carjacking law specifically gives the judge authority to stack the sentences, so you may have to finish serving one sentence before starting the next one. [39]

34. Why is carjacking being treated so severely by the lawmakers?

People have been murdered for refusing to give robbers their vehicles. Robbers have also stolen vehicles without realizing there were sleeping babies in them. Robbers have even caused tragic accidents while racing away from the scene of a carjacking. Lawmakers and society do not want to continue dealing with the loss of life at the hands of criminals who are willing to risk other people's lives for something as trivial as a vehicle.

Chapter 4

Bank, Safe, or Vault Robbery

35. What is bank, safe, or vault robbery?

Bank, safe, or vault robbery is any effort to commit larceny or any other felony that involves confining, injuring, threatening, scaring, intimidating, or compelling another person to in any way help or allow you to carry out the larceny or felony. Bank, safe, or vault robbery can also involve any attempt to break into or damage a bank, safe, or vault. [40]

36. How much time can you get sentenced to for bank, safe, or vault robbery?

The same as armed robbery or carjacking: imprisonment in the state prison for life or any term of years.

37. Can you still be convicted of bank, safe, or vault robbery if you only attempt but fail to actually succeed in the bank, safe, or vault robbery?

Yes. The law specifically addresses this, and it says you are guilty whether your attempt is a success or failure. [41]

38. Do you face less time if you do not physically assault anyone during the bank, safe, vault robbery?

Whether someone is physically assaulted or not, you will still face up to life in prison if you are convicted. [42] However, physical violence in any crime automatically increases one's odds of getting the most time permitted by law.

39. Can you get bank, safe, or vault robbery and armed robbery from a single incident?

According to People v. Witt, "the legislature intended to permit multiple punishments" for those crimes. [43] To be clear though, this means, while engaging in or attempting bank, safe, or vault robbery, the perpetrator also robs a person that is not working for or owning the bank, safe, or vault.

40. So if I robbed customers and bank tellers, I would get charged with armed robbery for robbing the customers and bank robbery for robbing the tellers?

Yes. [44]

41. Does the prosecutor have to charge me with bank robbery, or can I be charged with armed robbery for robbing a bank?

The prosecutor has the discretion to charge you with either. [45]

NOTES

1. MCLS 750.530 (1)

2. id.

3. MCLS 750.530 (2)

4. People v. Denny, 114 Mich. App. 320, 1982 Mich. App. LEXIS 3007 (Mich. Ct. App. 1982).

5. People v. Hicks, 259 Mich. App. 518, 2003 Mich. App. LEXIS 3026 (Mich. Ct. App. 2003).

6. People v. Hudson, 386 Mich. 665, 1972 Mich. LEXIS 211 (Mich. 1972).

7. People v. Martin, 37 Mich. App. 295, 1971 Mich. App. LEXIS 1210 (Mich. Ct. App. 1971).

8. People v. Mitchell, 32 Mich. App. 115, 1971 Mich. App. LEXIS 1850 (Mich. Ct. App. 1971).

9. People v. Williams, 28 Mich. App. 486, 1970 Mich. App. LEXIS 1208 (Mich. Ct. App. 1970).

10. See note supra 5.

11. People v. Passage, 277 Mich. App. 175, 2007 Mich. App. LEXIS 2551 (Mich. Ct. App. 2007).

12. id.

13. See note supra 3.

14. People v. Laker, 7 Mich. App. 425, 1967 Mich. App. LEXIS 592 (Mich. Ct. App. 1967).

15. MCLS 750.529; People v. Clark, 113 Mich. App. 477, 1982 Mich. App. LEXIS 2923 (Mich. Ct. App. 1982).

16. MCLS 750.529

17. People v. Halliburton, 114 Mich. App. 47, 1982 Mich. App. LEXIS 3169 (Mich. Ct. App. 1982).

18. People v. Wakeford, 419 Mich. 95, 1983 Mich. LEXIS 255 (Mich. 1983).

19. People v. Campbell, 165 Mich. App. 1, 1987 Mich. App. LEXIS 2926 (Mich. Ct. App. 1987).

20. People v. McCray, 17 Mich. App. 596, 1969 Mich. App. LEXIS 1256 (Mich. Ct. App. 1969).

21. People v. Jones, 71 Mich. App. 270, 1976 Mich. App. LEXIS 948 (Mich. Ct. App. 1976).

22. People v. Needham, 8 Mich. App. 679, 1967 Mich. App. LEXIS 519 (Mich. Ct. App. 1967).

23. People v. Kruper, 340 Mich. 114, 1954 Mich. LEXIS 330 (Mich. 1954).

24. People v. Lawson, 65 Mich. App. 562, 1975 Mich. App. LEXIS 991 (Mich. Ct. App. 1975).

25. People v. Martin, 75 Mich. App. 6, 1977 Mich. App. LEXIS 1071 (Mich. Ct. App. 1977).

26. People v. McGuire, 39 Mich. App. 308, 1972 Mich. App. LEXIS 1433 (Mich. Ct. App. 1972); People v. Ragland, 34 Mich. App. 624, 1971 Mich. App. LEXIS 1655 (Mich. Ct. App. 1971).

27. People v. Fisk, 62 Mich. App. 638, 1975 Mich. App. LEXIS 1101 (Mich. Ct. App. 1975).

28. People v. Banks, 454 Mich. 469, 1997 Mich. LEXIS 1279 (Mich. 1997).

29. People v. Henry, 315 Mich. App. 130, 2016 Mich. App. LEXIS 782 (Mich. Ct. App. 2016).

30. id; People v. DeMeyers, 183 Mich. App. 286, 1990 Mich. App. LEXIS 107 (Mich. Ct. App. 1990).

31. People v. Martin, 150 Mich. App. 630, 1986 Mich. App. LEXIS 2571 (Mich. Ct. App. 1986).

32. People v. Hogan, 9 Mich. App. 78, 1967 Mich. App. LEXIS 400 (Mich. Ct. App. 1967).

33. People v. Loncar, 4 Mich. App. 281, 1966 Mich. App. LEXIS 533 (Mich. Ct. App. 1966).

34. MCLS 750.529a (1)

35. People v. Parker, 230 Mich. App. 337, 1998 Mich. App. LEXIS 175 (Mich. Ct. App. 1998).

36. See supra note 34.

37. See supra note 34 (for carjacking sentence); see supra note 16 (for armed robbery sentence).

38. See supra note 34 (for carjacking sentence); see supra note 1 (for unarmed robbery sentence).

39. MCLS 750.529a (3)

40. MCLS 750.531

41. id.

42. People v. Ferguson, 60 Mich. App. 302, 1975 Mich. App. LEXIS 1441 (Mich. Ct. App. 1975).

43. People v. Witt, 140 Mich. App. 365, 1985 Mich. App. LEXIS 2439 (Mich. Ct. App. 1985).

44. People v. Ford, 262 Mich. App. 443, 2004 Mich. App. LEXIS 1492 (Mich. Ct. App. 2004).

45. People v. Thomas, 118 Mich. App. 667, 1982 Mich. App. LEXIS 3394 (Mich. Ct. App. 1982).

INDEX

Index numbers refer to question numbers, not to page numbers.

aiding and abetting: 25

asportation: 20

assault: 1, 4, 6, 10

bank, safe, or vault: 35-37, 39-41

carjacking: 26-29, 31, 33, 34, 36

fear: 1, 3-5, 8, 9, 16-18, 24, 26

fight: 6

force: 1, 3-5, 7-9, 16, 18, 24, 26

--attempting to escape from security at a store: 7

grabbing purses: 5

guilt by association: 6

intent: 21

intimidation: 9

larceny: 10, 35

"no one got hurt though": 5

possessing a dangerous weapon: 10, 19, 22-24, 27, 31

robbery: 14-16, 17, 19, 20, 25, 27, 28, 34

--aiding and betting: 25

--armed: 10-12, 19, 21, 23, 24, 27, 30, 36, 39-41
--directing others to move money or property: 20
--finger gun: 24
--grabbing purses: 5
--intimidation: 9
--multiple charges: 13, 39
--"no one got hurt though": 5
--planning robberies: 25
--robbing a business: 15
--robbing a diner: 9
--robbing a gas station: 21
--robbing banks, safes, or vaults: 35-37, 39-41
--stealing wallets at a bar: 6
--success or failure is irrelevant: 37
--threatening people: 17, 18
--unarmed: 1-9, 19, 23, 31, 33
--wrestling with security at a store: 8
sentences (concurrent v. consecutive): 33
stealing from a store: 8
threat of violence: 17, 18, 26
violence: 1, 4, 38
weapon: 10, 19, 22-24, 27, 32

Appendix

Waiver of jurisdiction when child of 14 or older is accused of felony

According to MCLS 712A.4, the law, "If a juvenile 14 years of age or older is accused of an act that if committed by an adult would be a felony [most crimes that are punishable by more than 1 year imprisonment], the judge...may waive jurisdiction [and] the juvenile may be tried in the court having general criminal jurisdiction of the offense." To waive the juvenile into the adult system, the court must (1) determine that the juvenile probably committed a felony and (2) determine that "the best interests of the juvenile and the public would be served by granting [the] waiver." This second part involves issues that relate to the seriousness of the offense, the juvenile's actual involvement in the offense, the juvenile's prior record, the juvenile's programming history, whether juvenile facilities will provide adequate punishment or programming, and other factors. If the juvenile is waived into the adult system, the juvenile will receive a lawyer if one is not already retained, and the juvenile will face adult court proceedings (e.g., jury selection, trial, sentencing) followed by release from custody or a sentence to prison time, which involves being transferred to prison and serving years there, until one completes the sentence, paroles, or dies.

Attention Reader

This book and all information provided in it is provided solely as the author's interpretation of select passages of Michigan law. Neither the author nor the text should be regarded as authoritative. For professional legal counsel, assistance, or information, readers should contact licensed legal professionals. In this publication, the author shares his thoughts about segments of law that he considers especially relevant to Michigan teens. In no manner should readers attempt to use material from this publication in place of professional legal counsel or assistance. Using this publication as a substitute for professional legal advice and assistance can result in severe legal consequences, which neither the author nor the publisher will be responsible for. Readers should discuss all legal concerns with qualified professionals prior to attempting any application of this text in any manner. This publication is an informal, non-professional, opinion-based publication that is published to draw readers' attention to the many serious consequences awaiting those who violate the law. This is not a professional legal publication, and again the author and publisher assumes no responsibility for how readers use the information provided herein.

www.ingramcontent.com/pod-product-compliance
Lightning Source LLC
Chambersburg PA
CBHW071618220526
45469CB00002B/392